THE COMMITTEE BOOK

Make your meeting smooth, enjoyable — *and* get things done!

Audrie Stratford

W. Foulsham & Co. Ltd.

London • New York • Toronto • Cape Town • Sydney

W. Foulsham & Company Limited
Yeovil Road, Slough, Berkshire, SL1 4JH

ISBN 0-572-01473-2

Printed in Great Britain
at St Edmundsbury Press,
Bury St Edmunds

CONTENTS

PREFACE

I embarked on this book about amateur Committee work because I could not find any adequate printed guidance on the subject and also because I have a lengthening history of serving on and learning about committees. Being by nature a 'joiner', I have long revelled in at least a couple of dozen memberships at any one time — unisex and mixed; centralised caring organisations which make no demands beyond the subscription; national pressure groups, their influence spread by international and local connections; local groups which apply pressure, give help or bring enjoyment. I have been in at the birth of one group and the death of another as well as experiencing all the phases between — growth, maturity, senescence and rejuvenation. Though I am now simply a member, I have done my share of Committee service and have acted in all main honorary offices, being grateful particularly to the London Association of University Women, the Western Australian Association of Women Graduates, the King's Lynn branch of the National Council of Women and the King's Lynn Society of Arts and Sciences for giving me such varied experience.

I was tossed into office as a wartime stop-gap, totally ignorant of what might be expected of me and believing that the absence of printed guidance was just another of the endless wartime shortages. I stumbled into pitfalls (most of them remembered in these pages) and was saved from countless more by the people around me, but even then I never quite grasped that the routines we were trying to administer were not necessarily 'right' (or 'wrong') but simply those which suited that particular set-up. So when, much later, I found myself wafted into the Chair the moment my election to it was announced and not at the end of that AGM as I had been expecting, I again looked for printed guidance, this time for justification of one or other of these two procedures. I found some books describing particular organisations in precise detail, others dealing with a particular office, a few seemingly intended for general application but worded so dogmatically that they implied that only those routines were right, and plenty dealing with statutory bodies. None of the books came near to solving any of my problems.

I then found that the problems were not mine alone. At a meeting of a Caring Association there was a chorus of agreement when one representative remarked that printed guidance would make her job rather easier by showing diffident people that Committee work and even office really were within their capabilities, particularly as it was usual to share Committee responsibility. Those carers, like so many other members of Committees up and down the country, were still expending time and energy trying to solve the same problems I had grappled with so long ago. Goodwill required that something should be done and the finger seemed to be pointing at me, especially as I had the critical support of Mrs Cecilia Whittley, to whom I am most grateful for rescue from plenty of infelicities.

I make no suggestion that good organisation is everything. If the target is not worthwhile, any project is likely to flounder, however good its routines; if its aims are worthwhile, it will probably be successful in the end but if the organisation is sloppy, the cost may be high in mental stress if not in money. It is when worthwhile aims are underpinned by carefully considered routines that an enterprise is most likely to succeed.

INTRODUCTION

Though a formal definition of a Committee is 'a body of people appointed for a special purpose by a larger body of people', you could describe it, less formally, as the most efficient way yet devised of helping any group to reach whatever target it has set itself. Committees are particularly successful when everything runs as if on oiled wheels, so this book sets out to supply the oil by describing essential group and Committee routines.

Most people believe that some Higher Authority has laid down a set of Universal Rules for Correct Group and Committee Procedures. Not so. There is not even any universally accepted title for what I shall call the Rules, but which might be called the Constitution or, perhaps, Bye-laws. Every group, large or small, devises whatever Rules best suit its own members and their plans. They are likely to be different from all others and because we do all tend to believe that our own ways are necessarily right, members soon come to think that any other ways are necessarily wrong. This cannot be so. Rules and procedures must be based on fundamental principles of human nature, on fair play and on common sense if they are to go on working. Therefore, different sets of Rules are sure to have much in common, but nothing in them is ever inherently 'right' or 'wrong'. That is why I have nowhere been dogmatic, for there is virtually nothing in the Committee world which is everywhere done in the same way. I have just described the ways which have stood the test of time and I try to show why they have done so.

It is unlikely that any group already practises every single relevant routine among those I have here described; different groups will have made quite different selections among those which were familiar to them, so I have done my best to cater for all needs and to give everyone some insight into why they do what they do — even if they also learn what they might do but don't! I have kept to feminine terminology in this book, partly because it seems likely that more women than men are 'joiners', but mainly in the same spirit as those writers who keep to masculine terminology even though their books, like this one, are meant to be used by both sexes.

A possible new Committee

A new Committee is on its way if you have got other people steamed up about an idea, possibly to keep an important footpath open, or to put on a play, for example. Probably, the idea needed initially a letter. Whoever writes it and deals with the answer becomes, in effect, the group's Secretary. The letter needs stationery and a stamp as well, so probably everyone chips in toward the cost and whoever looks after this 'kitty' (the Secretary or someone else) has taken on the job of Treasurer, at least temporarily. These two officers could probably run the group perfectly well on their own for quite a time but sooner or later a neutral, independent leader-figure is sure to be needed. This boss-person will probably be given the title first given way back when furniture was rare and costly and the only chair would be put at the disposal of the current leader who, therefore, became known as the Chair-man, a title often shortened (as so many terms now are) to 'Chair'.

As busier members of the group start leaving much of its activity to those of you who attend regularly, the basic Committee structure which I take for granted throughout this book develops automatically, with three main officers and a few of the more active people working on behalf of the membership as a whole. However, this Committee might embark on some project which the rest do not quite understand, so they become uneasy about it. Clearly, better two-way communication is needed so business

11

meetings get started. Then, to prevent later arguments, someone begins taking notes at the meeting and reading them back at the next meeting to make sure all are in agreement as to what was done. Your meetings are now being minuted. (In this context the word 'Minute' is pronounced as in the unit of time, not as for something very tiny. Please be kind to short thin Secretaries and use the title Minutes Secretary rather than writing about a 'minute secretary'!)

By now, most members are probably getting quite used to explaining to people what the group is trying to do. Inevitably, with repetition and your consultations together, wording will get more and more precise until it turns into a clear statement of aims. At the same time, you'll be clarifying your ideas of how the group ought to be run, how often you want to meet, how much you'll all subscribe to funds and so on. These ideas will become the first draft of your Rules.

Just one step more and the new group will have achieved a typical set-up. Any Committee acting on behalf of others and spending their subscription money is sure to worry about its responsibilities to those others. It will expect to report back to them at least once a year, summarising everything it has done since the previous equivalent meeting and asking members' approval of the year's work. A defined Financial Year becomes necessary and is among the first matters to get fixed as part of your Rules. That date will probably also settle the timing of the yearly 'tidying-up' meeting. The Annual General Meeting (AGM) is mostly held as soon after the end of the financial year as the checking of the Books of Account will allow so that the officers responsible for the function can be confirmed in office if they have justified themselves but if they have not, can be replaced before more harm is done. These things settled, the group really can think of itself as a functioning entity.

Compiling a set of Rules

Nowadays, most groups really get going at an exploratory meeting of as many as possible of those who think they might be interested. If enough are, the meeting appoints the Steering Committee, their most important task being the production of an acceptable set of Rules. These are as important to the smooth running of a group as a good Instruction Manual is to the smooth running of a piece of machinery and they need to be as precise and as meticulously followed. The job of compiling them is worth every moment spent on it, for without Rules no proper start can be made. Without proper Rules, smooth running is unlikely and Rules which are difficult to observe cause continuous problems. One exception made with the best of reasons and intentions often leads to another made lest feelings be hurt and gradually everything starts to run downhill. If this is already happening to a group you belong to, try to get them to make a fresh start with a new set of Rules based on what is in fact being done, after people have discussed what they, individually, are prepared to contribute to the group and what they, individually, want from it. Revised Rules of an established group can take effect as soon as they have been approved at a General Meeting. Once accepted, they should be kept.

Steering Committee

The work of a *Steering Committee* is speeded by using other people's experience so collect every set of Rules you can find, even if they seem different from those you are planning. Make full use of the advice scattered through this book and sort through all the various Rules you have collected, looking for anything which might be of use to your new Group. Arrange them in whatever order seems logical and will require least checking forward and backward; in short paragraphs (for easy quoting); numbered (for easy reference); with very concise wording (for easy understanding); precise (but defining words immediately or keeping to everyday meanings); and setting out in full the translation of any set of initials or any acronym on its first appearance (for people can become Committee members without having discovered the meaning of AGM or AOB). Legally-trained people can be helpful in suggesting ideas but beware of their terminology for they tend to use words in unexpected ways.

Help everything to get smoothly into gear by including in this first set of Rules a few interim clauses where necessary. For example, many groups protect Chair from undue weariness by setting a limit to her period of continuous service. If it happens that Chair of the Steering Committee becomes Founder Chair of the Group, should her permitted term of office be deemed to start at her appointment to the Steering Committee or her election by the Group? Whichever is decided, state it clearly in these first Rules so that the situation is known to all. Check through every proposed item for such potential hitches and cover them by interim or transitional clauses.

When you feel you have a workable version put it before a General Meeting. Carefully minute whatever wording is eventually agreed and add the date of that meeting. Get enough copies of this transitional version to last the existing membership a couple of years. The work of the Steering Committee is finished.

Accepted Rules

In due course, whether or not actual working has revealed weaknesses or gaps, review all the wording and practice. Remove the interim clauses which are not needed once the cycle is turning smoothly. Put this version before a formal General Meeting. If agreed, it needs only the addition of the date of that meeting to become the *accepted Rules* of the Group, suitable for a fullscale print-run.

Changes

Changes are sure to be needed eventually. Minute each as it is made and thereafter keep a minimum stock of copies of the Rules which have the changed version of the wording written or stuck in near the crossed-out original, and the date of the meeting which authorised the change. Alter only a few copies at a time for you may decide to change back. You would do well to keep among your records an up-to-date copy of the Rules with notes of every change made, dated to the Minute which authorised the change.

TYPES OF GROUP, TYPES OF MEMBER

If you are not burning to set up your own group but want to be part of one, search among those already established. There is usually plenty of choice in even quite small towns; in larger places the choice may be somewhat greater but the ideal group more difficult to identify. Start your search at the nearest centre of knowledge such as the local library or, perhaps, at the Citizen's Advice Bureau (CAB) or consult your local Directory of Services and Organisations. You will probably find that most of the well-known national organisations have branches not far away and there are sure to be many purely local groups. Usually the titles of these — Young Explorers, Silver Threads, Boxers All — will remove quite a lot of them from your list of possibles and may lead you directly to something which will suit you exactly. If no name especially attracts you, find out about the different groups' aims, not only as listed on paper but from members. Larger organisations often have quite a catalogue of targets but the particular selection of activities popular in your area may not be to your taste. Another organisation with apparently rather similar aims may work toward them in ways which suit you better.

There is no clear distinction between designations such as Federation, Association, Society, or between Branch and Club, but whatever the title, they boil down to just three main types of group.

Types of group

Entirely local
These do what they like, when they like; make and keep what money they can and spend it as they wish. They have

all the advantages but also the disadvantages of entirely independent action. For them I shall continue to use the term 'group'.

National organisations
These are often made up of local branches. The organisations will almost certainly be registered as non-trading limited liability companies and shown as such on their official publications. This gives certain advantages in law but imposes certain responsibilities, enshrined in their Articles of Association which, if only for the sake of all other members, must be meticulously observed by every member. I shall continue to use the word 'organistion' for them and use the term 'HQ' when distinguishing the central office from the organisation as a whole and from its branches or members. Organisations usually employ qualified advisors, so the main value of this book for them will be its reminders of the problems faced by the branches.

Local branches of national organisations
These have much in common with totally independent groups but there are many differences too, not least that the branches and their members are legally bound by the organisation's Articles of Association. Branches can look to their HQ for experienced advice and also for money to get established although, once established, they must help maintain HQ and *its* functions. Branches arrange their own fringe activities but their main work − collecting money, statistics, or whatever is their responsibility, or arranging meetings etc − is co-ordinated by HQ. If communication between centre and branches is good, the whole complex usually flourishes; if poor, local treasurers soon notice, for though contributions to HQ are set with the general agreement of representatives of all branches, it is actually paid by a levy on each individual member, the levy being known as a capitation fee (from the Latin *caput*,

a head). This forms such a large proportion of each sub-scription that anyone more interested in the fringe activities than in HQ's work is apt to jib at the large sums going out of the branch. On the other hand if people realise what good work is being done by HQ, they contribute gladly to it and usually help with the work as well.

Branches are usually independent enough for this book to be of help to them and I will go on applying to them the word 'branch' when distinguishing them from indepen-dent local groups.

Types of applicant

Not all applicants will become members. After all, you thought about whether or not the group might suit you and, fair's fair, a group must have the right to decide whether or not you might suit them. A few groups base their membership on selection. Some, such as musical societies, may have an entrance test. Some, such as Soroptimist International and Rotary, base their mem-bership on categories, so the group, knowing which categories are vacant, expects to take the initiative in inviting people to join.

Where there are no barriers of this type, refusal is unusual and anyone introduced by a member is almost guaranteed acceptance. However, the interests of estab-lished members must be considered as well as those of an applicant. If you were a member of a group would you be pleased if a skilled pickpocket had been accepted without demur, or an alcoholic, apt to become violent? That is why most sets of Rules state (and all assume) that the Commit-tee retains the right to refuse membership without giving reasons, especially as these might be libellous. If a com-plete stranger offers a subscription (which is, in essence, a token of membership) the Treasurer is well advised to express welcome, take particulars and ask that the request be renewed at the next meeting 'so that the application can be put before the Committee in accordance with our practice'. Only the ultra-touchy would take umbrage at this shifting of responsibility from the Hon Treasurer to the wider contacts of the Committee.

Types of member

Not even in the most egalitarian of groups are all members in the same category and many groups find that they can make their own routines easier by introducing sub-divisions of membership, so being able to offer it to a wider public. The division may be based on qualifications of one kind or another, on finance, or on responsibilities, the sections often overlapping. Each group determines for itself in its Rules whether sub-divisions affect rights to vote, to take office or to serve on the Committee. Confusing though this may sound, it is usually simple in practice.

Officers and Committee
Officers and Committee always have to be distinguished from the rest if only because of their greater responsibilities within the group. 'The rest' are sometimes referred to collectively as 'the floor' and individually as 'Ordinary Members'. As people they may be anything but ordinary so be careful, in this context, always to use the initial capital 'O'.

Linked interests
In groups which have two or more *linked interests*, such as an Operatic and Dramatic Society, members may find themselves on only one of the membership lists.

Associate Members
People with more limited qualification for membership than is expected in a particular group (eg Junior Members), or who have less easy access to the group's assets (eg Country Members of a metropolitan group)

may be acceptable as *Associate Members*. They usually have fewer rights and pay a lower subscription. Capitation fees, if any, are reduced pro rata (pronounced *pro RAH-ta*, from the phrase meaning 'at the same rate' ie 'in proportion to').

Retired Members
Retired Members, however defined, sometimes pay reduced subscriptions and capitation fees. They do not necessarily lose any rights, for they often have valuable experience to contribute and may be the only ones with time to do the group's work.

Married couples
Married couples or other pairs living at the same address occasionally retain all rights yet pay less than double, though more than a single, subscription between them.

Life Members
Life Members have chosen to pay one actuarially-determined lump sum which should, if invested, bring the group as much money as that member would be likely to pay in a lifetime of annual subscriptions. With inflation, life members became a financial liability and few groups now accept new ones.

Honorary Members
The smallest sub-division, and the most special, consists of *Honorary Members*. The word implies that no payment is involved (donations being a different matter). Just as an employed secretary is paid but an Honorary Secretary is not, so other members pay subscriptions but Honorary Members do not. Honorary membership is offered, not requested, for its purpose is to confer honour. Only honoured and honourable people are likely ever to be offered honorary membership but take care not to confuse the three words when voicing the title for it is usually abbreviated in print to 'Hon Member'. The rights and

duties of an Hon Member are likely to be different from those of any other members of that group and they differ widely from one group to another according to each particular set of Rules. Some might permit an Hon Member to serve on Committees, to hold office and to vote, even on financial matters; others would consider these to be totally undemocratic. And do remember, when considering inviting someone to become an Hon Member, that although all appreciate the honour conferred and the financial freedom, some may be reluctant to accept if it means losing rights of voting and serving.

There are other points your Rules should cover when defining honorary membership. How long is the membership in this special category to last? An Hon Member costs as much as any other and if she is elected for life, what happens when costs rise greatly? If for just a year, is the invitation renewable? Without limit? Who eventually tells her she must start paying? On whose instructions? Who elects her in the first place? Other questions arise if honorary membership is offered *ex officio* (pronounced *EKS off-FISS-ee-oh* from the phrase meaning 'by virtue of the office') as when the position is regularly offered to the incumbent Mayor of the borough for the term of the mayoralty.

All these possibilities should be thought through before you consider enrolling an Honorary Member, although the category has notable advantages. Some groups use it to honour an eminent person who lacks the particular qualifications they normally require; others use it to retain a valued member whose income has dropped. Such people are sometimes further distinguished by the title 'Hon Vice-President', which sounds so impressive and is so ill-defined that often the 'Hon' is omitted. I will refer again to this category when considering VIPs.

OFFICERS

There are only two essential qualifications for being an officer; you must be devoted enough to the group to sacrifice time and energy to it, and, enough members must believe that you are capable of taking on the responsibilities. Occasionally, when for the time being no others can be found who are willing and able to act, one person may hold two or even more of the offices but fundamentally there should be at least three people. Each of them when communicating with other groups writes to her own opposite number, Chair addressing Chair, Secretary writing to Secretary etc.

The responsibilities of office

Officially, officers are deemed to be the servants of the group and are usually recorded as having been 'instructed' to carry out certain actions; in practice, it is they who run the group. The responsibilities should not be taken lightly but should not be allowed to become onerous burdens. If you felt (or even were!) physically sick before your first time in the Chair, don't worry. The same thing has happened to almost every officer worthy the title. But if you continue to feel you are overburdened, make sure you get assistance of some kind. Martyrdom helps neither you nor the group.

Mental attributes

Mental attributes, as listed in many books on the subject, include leadership, good humour, integrity and other excellent qualities. Certainly these are desirable in officers as, surely, they are in everyone. But few groups are so rich in potential officers that individual characteristics can be the main basis of choice. In most cases the whole personality has to be considered, in the hope that successive officers will bring different qualities to the job. If people, otherwise apparently excellent, decline to stand for office for no other reason than that they fear defeat in the election, they should be persuaded to accept nominations, remembering that votes are cast for quite curious reasons. Very thin-skinned people should not be over-persuaded into standing, for office always brings a degree of criticism — which most people welcome as being potentially helpful to them.

Physical attributes

These are rarely of significance, but one — inaudibility — can be quite a menace. Some people, mainly women, have been brought up to believe they should not raise their voices, yet listeners to a quiet tone usually lower their own voices in unconscious mimicry. Plenty of people are at least slightly deaf, some believing it to be a kind of stigma to be kept secret. Most people are unwilling to ask anyone to speak up, so some meetings become more and more a hushed discussion among those sitting nearest the Chair. If members cannot rely on hearing what is said at a meeting, they lose interest.

Financial implications of office

No-one should be out of, nor in, pocket as a result of taking office. All who spend money on the group at its instruction or with its permission should expect and accept re-imbursement, recorded by the Treasurer as an expense. If you choose to return it as a donation, that is between you and the Treasurer, but it is mistaken generosity to forgo payment by claiming to be too busy to keep count of phone calls and stamps. If this becomes accepted practice sooner or later a potentially good officer will refuse nomination simply because she cannot afford to do the same.

Officers' 'combined operations'

The main officers should expect to act as a team holding informal officers' meetings to thrash out policy so that they can speak with one voice. Having discussed details, this saves time at members' meetings although of course the officers as a body must not take up entrenched positions. Sometimes one officer may take on a job usually done by another if it is to their mutual advantage, but no officer should take on a job which could as well be done by someone from 'the floor'. On social occasions officers do well to disperse themselves among members so as to be available for answering questions; also, they can break tactfully into incipient cliques and may even pick up informative rumours.

Length of officers' continuous service

Groups which need officers who know their activities and traditions inside out let them continue to serve for as long as they wish, even if it leads to problems when they ought to be replaced. In most groups, freshness of ideas and of contacts are more important than traditions, so most Rules set limits to their officers' continuous service. People generally seem more willing to accept nomination for a specified period than for a potential life sentence and to an office which they are sure will have been vacated rather than one which has an incumbent, however loudly she may proclaim her willingness to stand down. Fresh thoughts are more important in some offices than in others. A Treasurer rarely needs to modify her routines (except in money-raising groups) so generally she stays in office longer than a Secretary. Chair's term is usually the shortest, some Rules limiting her to one year. This lets more people share the experience and helps conserve Chair's energy and time (though most could pace themselves and, even with the shortest of terms, none can guarantee free time, for that depends upon the demands of other people). But a Chair needs to seem confident, which may be difficult as long as she is on unfamiliar ground, and without at least a second term, neither group nor Chair will benefit from lessons learnt in her first year.

Officers' official records and supporting papers

Each main office has its own official set of books, guarded by the incumbent officer during her period in office then passed to her successor. Chair can be held responsible for the legal documents such as the Rules, as well as any particular non-documentary valuable such as the branch insignia; Treasurer is in charge of the whole range of books of financial accounting, and Secretary responsible for records of agreed decisions, usually called the Minutes books.

On taking office you should immediately check that you have received all the books and papers listed as your responsibility. Some may be photocopies only, the originals being 'banked' with other archives in some safe place. At the end of your period in office check your books against the same list then pass all to your successor with an up-to-date list, for you may have added something fresh. When you first get the books, glance through the more recent entries to find what activities have been actually set in motion and which have merely been discussed. As soon as convenient after that, read right through to get a complete picture of the job.

Later I describe how each set of records is kept. You will see that the traditional ways have still not been bettered for amateurs, being surprisingly user-friendly and ensuring that responsibility never has to be borne by one person alone but is widely shared. Newcomers to office often yearn for modern loose-leaf methods but be very wary of these. In amateur hands they are always suspect. Most such records are marred by gaps where someone has, for a presumably good reason, removed and failed to return one or more pages. Such sheets are easily lost; the gap is almost undetectable and, once lost, the information is irreplaceable. Amateur groups which value their archives should guard against these easy removals by keeping all records fixed in bound books, the pages numbered prior to use, the books themselves listed.

You are sure to inherit some of your predecessor's correspondence and may wonder how long you ought to retain letters and carbon copies. To a great extent each officer must make up her own mind but before you do, discuss the matter with the Committee and get the decisions minuted.

Officers' unofficial diaries

Anyone who has served on a Committee knows something of each officer's work but not necessarily the individual quirks of a particular office at a particular moment, quirks which make short-notice replacement so difficult. There will be less risk of panic if you (and all who are doing a job for the group) keep the essential dates, addresses, phone numbers and other relevant data filed with the diary of the job. Start to write or update it as soon as you first take office, making sure you include every item you wish someone had warned you about and every one they did, as well as any which may have seemed general knowledge but which you had to find out for yourself. Once compiled, the diary can be passed onto whoever takes over the job, temporarily or permanently. As long as you do it yourself, the diary becomes an excellent memory-jogger and if after a break you return to the job believing you know the routine, an up-to-date diary may well save you from many a gaffe by showing that there have been changes since your day.

The 'scrap book'

The 'scrap book' is the name used to describe the group's collection of printed ephemera. This is among the most important of the group's records, illustrating vividly the interface between the group and the reading public. It should include every printed reference, in words or pictures, to the group as a whole or any of its members and although the details may be wildly inaccurate, that is part of the interest. The book should also include everything printed by the group for distribution to any part of the public — tickets, handbills, menus for invitation dinners and much besides. The most suitable book is in A4 format, with blank pale pages to allow of easy annotation. Beside each entry there should be a note of the occasion, the origin of the cutting, photo or paper, with the date (of the publication, not necessarily the event) and, if relevant, a crossreference to the programme. If a glossy original photo is available as well as the printed version, identification names could be written direct on the latter. Now that newsprint degenerates so fast, original cuttings are safest packed away in the dark after photocopies have been taken for sticking (with archive quality adhesive) into the scrap book so that they are safe from casual removal.

These fascinating records have not yet fitted themselves into any of the three sets of officers' records (the undignified name being no help). But guardianship of the 'scrap book' is an important job which in a small group is likely to be undertaken by an officer but which should be passed as soon as possible to someone from 'the floor'. It is often the only job which can be undertaken by a member who is temporarily or permanently unable to attend meetings but who wishes to remain in active contact. It is also unusual in that there is no recognised routine for authenticating the work, checking that it is reasonably complete, of taking group responsibility for it or even for passing on the book. It is important that every group should devise a routine for checking that the scrap book is kept up-to-date, one of the best being to display it regularly as part of the AGM and all other important meetings.

Officers' aides

As groups grow and undertake more activities, the main officers often need help in their jobs, some preferring an all-purpose assistant to lend a hand wherever needed, others preferring a specialist to take complete responsibility for some particular part of the job, eg a Minutes Secretary. Unfortunately there is no consensus about the implications of the various titles given to officer's aides. Current Rules may be helpful but 'job requirements' should always be discussed with any suggested nominee so as to make it clear whether, for example, officer status is implied. People feel sore if they think they have been invited to do a certain job and find themselves expected to do something quite different.

A deputy officer

A deputy officer is usually taken to be an understudy, often elected for the same maximum term as her main officer and subject to much the same conditions. She is expected to learn about the main office and be ready to take it on at short notice, for a brief or longer period. Members watch a deputy to see if she is sufficiently capable of doing the job to deserve re-nomination or, if Rules allow for two simultaneous deputies, which of them would be the better in the main job. The deputy, meanwhile, is finding out whether she wishes to take on the main job. If she does not, she should not accept re-nomination as deputy (certainly not as sole deputy) for that implies willingness to serve in the main office in due course.

Acting officer

An Acting officer is generally agreed to be a full but temporary replacement, possibly because the position could not be constitutionally filled at that time but sometimes because no-one suitable could be found to accept the full responsibility of the main office.

Vice-President and Vice-Chair

These titles (for Vice-Secretary and Vice-Treasurer seems not to exist) are such confusing titles that they are best avoided entirely for, being mistranslations, they have no guaranteed meanings. The prefix 'Vice-' is derived from the phrase meaning 'in full place of'. It is most exactly illustrated by its direct derivative 'vicarious' and exemplified by the job of Viceroy (in full place of the king or queen). However, in Committee parlance it is sometimes taken to mean the same as 'deputy' as if the Prince of Wales were to be called the Viceroy. The confusion between the terms Deputy and Vice- may have arisen from a natural desire to give a hard-working officer a grand title, linked with vague memories of the far grander title of *Hon* Vice-President, which I have referred to later.

Officer elect

This title is not often seen but can be precisely defined — time, for once, being of the essence. The terms are only applicable when the Rules stipulate an interval between the declaration of election results and the assumption of office of those elected. The most familiar example is that of the American President. Between Election and Inauguration Days everyone knows who will next hold office but that person gains no official powers at all until inaugurated.

Peripheral jobs

In small groups, everyone, officers included, must perforce lend a hand with almost every activity and possibly be in direct charge of several. In larger groups this is inefficient. Officers should not be hidden away, perhaps making coffee, but out in front, concentrating on their jobs as officers (even putting their visitors into the care of other members to make sure that both job and visitor get undistracted attention). Handing over peripheral jobs to 'the floor' is in the group's long-term as well as immediate interest for it is usually by successfully tackling minor jobs that people prepare themselves for higher office.

Hostess

Everyone, officer or not, should certainly make strangers and new members welcome but an official *hostess*, free from other responsibilities and expecting to spend time explaining what is going on and making introductions is a great asset and she will, incidentally, become an authority on members' names and interests.

Sick visitor

Many groups appoint a *sick visitor*. The job calls for more than sympathy and a car. She needs, for example, to remember that people living alone rarely welcome visitors who are unheralded and though some invalids yearn for flowers and gossip, others dread both.

First aiders

At small meetings, the disturbance and alarm caused by sudden illness is reduced by a knowledge of which members are *first aiders* who can be relied upon to cope or to call for other help. This lifts a real, though almost subconscious, load from everyone. (At large, or public, meetings, when no member should be distracted from the business in hand, a Red Cross or St John's uniform is a comforting sight. These organisations make no charge but do not refuse donations or invitations to join in the meal or the entertainment.)

'Look-out'

Officers can carry on relatively calmly through minor disturbances — persistent phone calls or casual police visits, for example — if they are confident that someone present is expecting to act as *'look-out'* and take the lead in dealing with any situation.

Transport officer

People are very reluctant to beg lifts for themselves so a *transport officer* can build up a fund of goodwill by matching empty car seats with potential walkers and may, in doing this, increase the numbers willing to attend evening meetings.

Officials

Officials are the full- or part-time employees of a group — Secretary, golf pro, drama coach, embroidery adviser — their job descriptions being very different from those of officer. Officers are always voting members, are elected and unpaid whereas officials are appointed (often by officers), paid, and protected by national laws concerning holidays, conditions of work, etc, which might be ignored by the employee herself but which could be invoked on her behalf by third parties.

Officials might not have the precise qualifications required for membership of the organisation they work for so though most do join, their membership cannot be taken for granted and officials, as such, have no further place in this book.

CHAIR AND OTHER VIPs

Chair

It could be said that whoever is in the Chair is ultimately responsible for everything the group does. The buck stops with you. The brickbats will have your name on them and so, too, will the bouquets. However, don't let this sweeping statement worry you too much. It is really just a reminder that Chair's range of activities is so wide and so different from one group to another that it cannot be described in detail and, more than any other office, it has to adapt to immediate needs. In an emergency you may find yourself doing a quite menial job simply because it had to be done immediately and everyone else seems occupied (and you'd better make sure someone else is responsible for that job in future). Having done it, you must immediately revert to your position of pre-eminence for this one generalisation can be made about your job as Chair. However shy you may be as a person, you owe it to your office never to be selfeffacing. You should always be easily identifiable, ready for anything; at business meetings and lectures, the pivot of all activity; at social meetings, either near the entrance to be the first to greet visitors or, having left a deputy to do that, moving among the guests, accepting the deference due to your office whether or not to you as a person.

Make sure other officers get things done within the Rules of your group and in their own ways. Delegate to them as many jobs as you can for they and the Committee will feel frustrated if you keep all the action to yourself. In the same way, make sure they shed as many minor jobs as possible to officers' aides or to 'the floor' to prevent members from feeling left out.

Your most important work will be done between

meetings. Inevitably you will soon know more than anyone else about the group and will be doing most of the planning for the future, making contacts, warning, guiding, tending new ideas and holding everything together in amity. However, it is as the Chair of a meeting that you will be most often seen. You will find this job has much in common with solo hostessing of a dinner party. Chair and hostess both have their event planned on paper (agenda and menu) and both assume that those present will behave with public good manners though each knows that if anyone, through political motivation or sheer ignorance, causes disruption, she will have to cope on her own. When, at big events, they need to win silence both use some form of gavel (or, preferably, gong or bell, for these sound pleasanter and can be either gentle or loud). Both are for the time being paramount and both must be, or at least seem, cool and neutral. (At a push, if her feelings are deeply aroused, Chair has a get-out not shared by the hostess. She can ask someone else to take her place for that one item while she has her own, un-neutral, say.) Both encourage others to do the talking but their very different aims are shown by the habitual seating arrangements. The hostess seats her guests around dining tables to encourage the enjoyment of general conversation; Chair keeps her members facing toward her, usually in rows so that each can hear everything said by everyone. Both appreciate the occasional moments of reversal, a hostess being happy when most talking stops for a moment and heads are craned toward a particularly interesting speaker; Chair, knowing that when people are flummoxed by a new idea they may need to mull it over in groups, sometimes lets them do this before calling them to order again.

A hostess (or host) is not essential for a group meal but if a meeting is ever to get going, there must be someone (not necessarily any particular person, but someone) in the Chair. If at a Committee Meeting neither Chair nor any of her official deputies is present, the members would soon decide who was most qualified to act and informally invite her to do so. At a larger meeting the same result would be differently reached. Responsible people would put their heads together, discuss who, among those present, seemed most likely to cope well with the emergency and then put the problem to her. Only if she is really not free is she justified in refusing to act. Having agreement, any one of the concerned people, staying on the floor, silences the members and says, loudly but not to anyone in particular, something like 'Miss Woodhouse has had a slight accident and cannot be with us today. I propose that Mrs Weston be asked to take the Chair'. Someone else says 'I second that' and, unless there is a sustainable objection, all present should chorus 'Hear, Hear'. Mrs Weston goes to the platform, calls the meeting to order and does her best, including among other business Miss Woodhouse's apologies for absence. Throughout the meeting, Mrs Weston is referred to and addressed as 'Mme Chair'.

Apart from such emergencies try, toward the end of your stint, to be unavoidably absent from an occasional meeting which you know your deputy will be attending and must, therefore, Chair. It is another stage in her training for office.

In discussing your hopes and difficulties with your officers you, as Chair, will be aware of their problems but they do not necessarily share all yours. You may feel the need for advice from someone who has no specific responsibilities on this Committee but does know how much tender loving care all groups need from their top officers. This usually implies a public figure. People of this eminence are known in various groups by various titles and they expect various rights and responsibilities which also vary from group to group so if they are not yet defined in your Rules avoid issuing any invitation until you have discussed the details within the group and have incorporated the wishes of the majority in the Rules. For example, will she be deemed an officer? Must she already be a member? What if she is not even eligible for normal membership? By what route should she be invited? For how long? Renewable? Without limit? For life? Which meetings will she have the right to attend? Which to speak at? Which take the Chair at? Which vote at? Should there be any financial obligations either way? Will the title of the functioning Chair be changed? (Sometimes it is altered to Chair of Committee.) What title will be used for the higher adviser?

Patron

A 'Patron' is mostly, though not exclusively, royal. Such eminence does not come within the ambit of this book. The people usually known as patrons because they patronise the productions of performing societies are not, in any sense, officers' advisers.

President

This title is sometimes given to an officer who functions in all ways as Chair, the prestigious sound presumably supposed to be some compensation for the ardours of the job, although, as the list of officers will show no Chair as such, the true position is not really disguised.

A President, functioning in addition to a Chair, is always her own person, chosen for her own particular qualities, so that a deputy would be unthinkable. She may be of near-Patron eminence or may be even less well-known than Chair herself but she can bring much to the group, especially advice, contacts and status.

When Presidents are appointed *ex officio* (eg a Mayoress) some become quite dedicated to the work of the group but others are totally uninterested, so when Rules include *ex officio* appointments, routines must be devised which will apply as smoothly when the President takes part as when she does not.

Vice-President

Some groups list a Vice-President among their officers and many organisations name several Hon Vice-Presidents on their notepaper, yet most people are vague as to the precise implications of the title. This is hardly surprising for it is used in two quite different ways. Sometimes it is applied as a synonym for Deputy Chair to whatever member is understudying the Chair she expects later to replace. In other organisations the title is offered to eminent people, not necessarily even technically qualified for membership, in gratitude for work they have done, possibly in some quite different sphere. This kind of Vice-President is chosen for her own personality. She can have no deputy and is not herself deputy to anyone in that organisation.

Immediate Past Chair

Some sets of Rules include the Immediate Past Chair in their Committee structure, perhaps for just one year to ease an inexperienced Chair into office, perhaps until she is no longer Immediate Past Chair. The arrangement is useful in ensuring an immediate and willing source of advice and in reducing risk of total loss of continuity when Rules require that everyone on the Committee must offer herself annually for re-election. However, not every Chair likes having her immediate predecessor breathing down her neck.

A Past Chair is only considered as a functioning officer if all other deputies are absent but the possibility of this . prolongation of service should be borne in mind when an invitation to stand for the office of Deputy Chair is first received.

Past Chair

This is an imprecise term. When Rules refer simply to a 'Past Chair' and the Immediate Past Chair is not avail-

Chair's Agenda is, as the example shows, a version of the main list but amplified by the addition of data she might need. She will not necessarily make use of all the notes but better a name written down and not used than an essential name forgotten. Let's deal with the main items in turn.

1) 'Welcome by Chair.' At a Committee meeting, Chair will probably have greeted people individually. With this item she signals the formal start of the meeting and sets its tone. She may also use the item to congratulate one or commiserate with another and, at general meetings, by her welcome to a visitor may account for a strange face. Occasionally she may speak of her particular pleasure in having represented the group at some event. This last will probably come from her own memory; the other reminders should be on her particular Agenda sheet.

2) 'Apologies for absence.' These matter at Committee meetings where the total number of potential attenders is known. As soon as the number of apologies added to the number present equals the total number expected, the meeting may as well start, whatever the time. At general meetings it is usually only those who were due to play some part who send a message unless total numbers are small or Rules require members either to put in a certain number of appearances or account for their absences.

3) 'Minutes of the meeting held on . . . .' This means the previous (not, we hope, the last) equivalent meeting. If not reprographed and circularised they should be read aloud uninterrupted.

4) 'Matters arising' is the usual heading for this item but sometimes it is more descriptively worded 'Minor matters arising from the Minutes and not included elsewhere'. There is an alternative way of numbering this, too. The item is so closely linked with the previous one that in some

lists they are numbered 3a) and 3b). Most people, however, find that there is already so much sub-division of items in the setting out and writing up of records that further sub-division ought to be avoided where possible.

Item 3) gave opportunity for Minutes to be read out without any interruption as a record of what actually happened at the Meeting. Item 4) (or 3a) according to the numbering system chosen) is the place for interjections, explanation and elaborations. Had it not been included in the Agenda, people might have heard, at some point in the reading 'Treasurer was instructed to ask the Mayor . . . (but I know she didn't because they were both ill just then) . . .'. Separation aids clarity.

As you go through the previous Minutes or are told of problems, prepare to list them all on Chair's Agenda, identifying each with the number of its occurrence in the original Minutes. At the meeting, Chair will deal with all the points you have listed on her Agenda then ask if anyone wishes to take up any other points, points which may not have been known to you. This is not the time to re-hash old arguments so do not make any unnecessary references but all doubts should be eliminated now, by someone, and all of them summarised in the next Minutes. If any one of the explanations is likely to be complicated or is part of another item on the Agenda it should be deferred until that item is reached and listed there on Chair's Agenda.

5), 6), and 7) 'Officers' Reports and Correspondence'. The purposes of these items is to bring members absolutely up-to-date with all aspects of the group's activities. But in what order should they be taken? Need all be included? When there is rarely much correspondence or almost all of it belongs to the work of the Secretary or Treasurer, the item 'Correspondence' is sometimes omitted from the Agenda. You can find out what is customary in your group by consulting earlier

Minutes. These will also show who usually speaks first, Secretary or Treasurer. The Secretary often has more, and more varied, information to give than Treasurer has, and might be expected always to speak first but most groups, liking to know how much cloth they have before considering the cut of the coat, expect to hear first from the Treasurer. This has the incidental advantage that if the Secretary has read the Minutes a change of voice will be welcome. But all officers should be circumspect in their demeanour especially when they are not speaking. No-one should ever seem other than deeply interested in what is being said, however familiar it might be.

8) and following. All are now as 'genned-up' as they ever will be to start discussing the future. Each group has its own special activities so the rest of the Agenda will differ widely from one group to another. Try to make sure the consideration of these special activities continues to develop in logical order but what that order is, this book cannot tell you.

The final item is usually called 'Any other business' (AOB). Occasionally the wording 'Other business by Leave' is used but it sounds so grudging that it is not to be encouraged. The item itself must always be included. The Agenda should have allowed for every item known to you when you typed it and perhaps nothing has arisen since but there might have been excitements galore, even at the last moment, so this place must be kept available for them.

AOB also gives opportunity to express gratitude. Anyone who has helped at the meeting deserves to have her name mentioned and, to make sure no-one is forgotten, you should have listed them on Chair's Agenda.

Write the date and place of the next meeting as part of the final item or just below it to remind a possibly exhausted Chair to give it out before declaring the meeting closed.

Minutes Secretary

This is usually the first job to be shed by an overbusy Hon Secretary. It would suit a Committee member who appreciates words and who cares about accuracy of detail. A copy of the Chair's Agenda can be very helpful but shorthand is only marginally an asset.

However unorthodox, the best way of learning the Do's and Don'ts of Minuting is to have searched through imperfect Minutes for precise information. The item may have seemed too unimportant to have been recorded or the wording may be almost without meaning. 'The letter from the Mayor was read out and discussed. It was decided to do nothing about it' may have seemed at the time to be an adequate summary of what was done but a later reader can only wonder who was Mayor and of where. Did the letter contain congratulations or reproof, offer help or refuse it? When you compose your Minutes, do so with a future reader very much in mind. Try always to get the very nub of the matter, taking special care whenever exact wording is important and including rather than omitting names. If formal propositions are made and decided by vote, proposer and seconder should be named and the number of votes stated. If, during a discussion, a member says 'I would like my protest Minuted, please', write it verbatim (pronounced *ver-BATE-im*, from the Latin *verbum*, a word, and meaning 'exactly word for word') and read out what you have written to make sure the protester and everyone else agrees it was the statement made. Almost certainly it represents either a reaction to a majority decision which is contrary to her known and deeply-held beliefs or she is preparing to say 'I told you so' and wants to be in a position to prove it.

Minutes should always pin responsibility precisely by recording who is to do what by when and when she is to report back to whom. Some groups who circularise their Minutes even emphasise this by using an extra column or a highlight pen to remind individuals of actions they should have taken.

Minuting any meeting falls into the same distinct stages.

Before and at the meeting

Prepare your notebook, a strong one, dedicated to the one job and kept tidily, for however rough the notes, they have the authority of immediacy and may at any time be called upon as evidence if the Minutes themselves seem inadequate.

Head a fresh page with the date of the meeting and, if it varies, the place. People do remember place more vividly than time and will more easily pinpoint a decision if reminded that it was 'taken in Mary's kitchen' than if told it was 'at the meeting last March' (or, on the international scene, 'at Helsinki' rather than 'at the 1980 triennial').

At a Committee meeting note down each member's arrival and the time the meeting started. All general meetings should start at exactly the scheduled time (no matter who has not yet arrived); if it is your custom to record numbers, count heads inconspicuously or, if you maintain one, get them from the attendance book. Note down the time of closure of all meetings.

Try to record more of the discussion than you expect to use, for until the meeting is finished, you cannot tell which points will be significant. Record everything in the order it happened, even if that is not the order of the Agenda because an officer had to leave early perhaps. When writing up your Minutes, record any such changes, for they may affect the interpretation of the discussion.

Very occasionally you may be called upon to cope with a break in the meeting. If too much business has been planned, or outside circumstances have forced an early closure, it may be impossible to finish the Agenda in one sitting. At some suitable moment, Chair will suggest a date and time for continuing the discussion and announce the ending of this first part not by closure but by adjournment. Make a conspicuous note of this in your book. If you are wise you will draft a record of this first part according to your normal routine. When the meeting is resumed (for it is still the same meeting, following the original Agenda), compile a new list of members present and the new time and place but otherwise just continue your notes. You will need to be extra alert when writing up, for arguments can be half-forgotten between the parts of such a meeting yet it is only at the actual closure of any meeting that the decisions taken at it become valid. Sometimes, even when no adjournment is involved, apparently firm and sensible resolutions may, later in the meeting, be seen to be unwise or impossible and have to be rescinded (pronounced *re-SIND-ed*, meaning 'repealed', 'cancelled').

Very occasionally a meeting is adjourned *sine die* (pronounced *SIGH-knee DYE-ee*, from the phrase meaning 'until such time') implying that no time or place is suggested for the resumption of the meeting, usually because no-one expects that it ever will be continued, though as it has not been formally closed it can be re-opened at any time.

Later

Start, as soon as possible, to change your notes into Minutes. Even one night's sleep will remove the memory of some details or later events affect your attitude to the business done and therefore to your choice of words. Unless you are very experienced you will almost certainly make several drafts, each a little clearer, more formal, concise, well-phrased, better arranged. Show the final one to the Chair of that meeting. If she interpreted something differently it is better to get it sorted out now than at the meeting.

Writing up the Minutes

If they are being circularised, include in the heading the type of meeting (Committee or General) for the benefit of those who receive sets of Minutes from various types of meeting, and the place, date and time. Next, for

Committee Meetings, name those who took part, starting with the Chair (if an Acting Chair, put her main office in brackets after her name) then the others in alphabetical order of surname, offices in brackets after names. End with your own name as the person responsible for the Minuting. For General Meetings, give just the Chair's name and yours as being the officers responsible for those Minutes.

Summarise the business done in accordance with the traditions of your group. Some like every possible detail recorded, some only the decision; some comment when discussion did take place, some only when it did not. Write impersonally, always including all data needed to allocate responsibility, for example, 'It was agreed that the Hon Treasurer should consult the Town Clerk about the terms for hiring the Assembly Rooms for the August lunch and report back to the May meeting' will be more helpful to everyone than 'we decided to check with the Town Hall'.

Final version

However this is produced, make sure there is space at the bottom (of every page if looseleaf) for the eventual dated signature. If your group has access to facilities, reprograph the Minutes ready for posting. Send them either immediately, while memories are still fresh or, more economically, delay until the next Agenda can go with them.

Less wealthy groups usually stick their single typed copy onto the numbered pages of the strongly bound Minutes Book, but some copy the record direct into the book in a fair hand. This last is easier on the binding of the book but if you do follow this practice, get everything checked for legibility by someone who did not help in the compilation. This will incidentally benefit future readers, but may save your own blushes in the shorter term if someone else has to read them out at the meeting. It is no credit to you if she can't!

Just before the next meeting

Someone, probably you, should check through the Minutes to find whether anyone needs chivvying. At the same time make a list, including an identifying number, of every item which ought to be mentioned as one of the 'matters arising', ready to be put on the Chair's Agenda. If, while doing this, you find any mistakes, cross each out neatly, write the correct version nearby and initial the change. Erasures should not exist in official records.

At the next equivalent meeting

These Minutes will be read as item 3) — Committee Minutes at the Committee meeting, General Minutes at the General meeting. The same matters may well have been discussed in both streams of meetings but different people being at the two discussions, the arguments may have developed differently so bring all recent notes and record books to all business meetings in case anything needs cross-checking.

Make sure that all stages of the acceptance of Minutes, as well as their compilation are taken seriously. If they have been reprographed, Chair will probably say 'May we take these Minutes as read?', a proposal which is usually agreed for it saves much time. Assent implies and should mean that they have been read. When not circularised, as, for instance, those of general business meetings, read them out, slowly and distinctly. Usually the only real problem is the reading of lists of members. The English language is plagued by a lack of acceptable plurals for its personal titles Mrs, Miss, Ms, Mr. A possible solution is to write them in full but read surnames only.

After the reading, Chair will ask 'Does everyone agree that this is a true record of the meeting?' Disagreement does not cast a slur on the Minutes Secretary, who has much to distract her. It would be a greater slur if inaccurate Minutes compiled by her were accepted so every apparent inaccuracy should be pointed out. Memories and notes must be searched until agreement is reached. If the written version was inaccurate, neatly cross out the mistake and write in the new agreed version nearby. This time it is Chair who initials the alteration to guarantee it. You will Minute the number of changes, for example, 'The Minutes were read and after two minor corrections, accepted', so that the crossings out tally with the record, making tampering unlikely. If, by any mischance a really lengthy alteration has to be made, perhaps because you copied a wrong excerpt, do not waste time by trying to correct it immediately. Instead, note the problem and include the correct version in the next Minutes, for acceptance then.

Acceptance of Minutes should be unanimous so when it seems that all are agreed, Chair doublechecks by asking 'Is there anyone who does not agree this is now a true record?' Last or first (and it usually is first) the time comes when all are agreed. Chair signs (every page if looseleaf) and dates her signature. The date is the one which should head the next set of Minutes in the book, making it easy for the completeness of the sequence to be checked.

That signature changes the status of that set of Minutes. They are no longer your personal account of that meeting but part of the recorded history of that group or Committee, accepted as such by everyone there and attested by the signature of the Chair. It is to achieve this status that the preceding ritual has been developed. Meanwhile, Chair will be looking to her Agenda for the Matters expected to arise and you will be continuing your next set of notes.

Programme Secretary

This job, which an over-busy Secretary is usually glad to delegate, is very satisfying for someone who likes to work on her own and is good at detail.

Things will go most smoothly if you start by getting a full and accurate 'job description'. Are you expected to arrange just lectures for members? or to arrange all their meetings? including AGMs and parties? What about

Regional or Open meetings? Who books rooms, you or the Hon Treasurer? Who corrects programme proofs, you or the Hon Secretary? Will there be a sub-committee to help you? Will you be responsible for arrangements on the day itself? (There is less scope for confusion if you are) What kind of budget will be allowed? Who is supposed to suggest themes? Speakers? Subjects? Have any speakers been contacted prior to your taking over? Is anything actually fixed? Who makes which decisions? Dates, venues, pick-up points for coach outings (few subjects generate more discussion), 'holidays' (at one time, August was virtually free from meetings because everyone was away but with longer travel seasons, July, August and September meetings tend to be equally, or equally thinly, attended). What is the annual rhythm of the programmes? If the send-outs are seasonal or annual, things become very hectic for a month or so before circularisation and if this time includes a holiday season, frustration can become maddening, but at least on the other hand hardly anything needs to be done for most of the rest of the year. If meetings are individually arranged and circularised, the activity is spread more evenly, but there is rarely a real let-up and the printing will cost rather more.

Booking a speaker

Before you get right down to this, make absolutely sure that the meeting room is booked for all the relevant dates. Then have a word with your regular printer to find out about deadlines. Working back from the date of the first meeting on the programme, decide how much notice for it the members will expect and, from this and your knowledge of the time taken to get notices out to members, judge the last date for receiving the finished programme from the printers. They can allow for holidays and regular annual commitments and, knowing these, will stipulate when they must have the final approved copy. Always ask for proofs, not in criticism of the printer's excellence, but because your own mistakes show up much more vividly in print than in your own familiar writing. The making, supplying, correcting and returning of proofs all take time, so the date the printers will suggest as your deadline is already surprisingly near. You'd better get on with the bookings. Most people start by making a programme diary, a large piece of paper ruled into as many spaces as there are to be meetings, each space labelled with one of the scheduled dates and filled in if any arrangements have been completed. Then consider your first suggested speaker.

The best preliminary, if this is practicable, is to phone her. Introduce yourself, your group and your purpose, then investigate whether she can be available on the suggested date and whether the group can afford her costs — fees, hire of equipment, transport with meals and taxis en route, accommodation (occasional speakers tend to like staying with members, professional speakers prefer hotels, though they cost you a lot more). If, during the discussion, anything proves awkward, either side can withdraw gracefully. If all goes well, take the opportunity to get other details checked, especially finding out exactly what equipment she will need and how much of it she can bring with her. Rely on her for as much of this as possible for slide carousels are best filled at leisure in the speaker's own home and she is sure to feel easier with familiar paraphernalia. (And, of course, it may save group funds.)

This is also a good moment to investigate alternative dates (just in case some other speaker has to request a change) and to explain what length of talk is expected and whether there will be a business meeting before or after it. Always give some description of the type and likely size of audience. Speakers take in their stride the effects on numbers of winter colds or summer holidays but are not pleased if faced with a couple of hundred youngsters after preparing a talk appropriate to a couple of dozen pensioners.

Find out how the speaker's name should be pronounced and make a note to warn everyone just before the meeting of the usage she will expect. At the same time, ask members not to try being funny about her name or her job. Manners apart, she will have heard all the jokes, ad nauseum, just as most women's groups get tired of hearing a male speaker trying to be funny about the 'newly acquired harem' around him. Finally, promise to send, by a specified date, a letter of confirmation of all details. Rejoicing in the satisfactory results of that conversation you can pencil into the diary the name and subject and any special warnings and comments. Then start on the same procedure with the next person on your list.

Before the date promised, send the confirmatory letter. Make it the basis of a full exchange of information. Mention again the length of talk expected and say whether or not the room has a clock clearly visible to the speaker or whether it is the audience who can see it. Ask for written confirmation of the exact title of the talk and the spelling of the surname, the titles and initials or given name of the speaker and any relevant qualifications exactly as these are to appear on the programme. Send maps showing the meeting hall and car parks or BR station (and a timetable) and also a copy of an earlier programme to indicate the style and level of talk expected. If possible include some literature outlining the work of the group, for always a surprising number of people have never heard of even the best known organisations yet may wish to make tactful references to its activities. Include, also, a stamped, self-addressed envelope (SAE) and state a date by which you will be expecting to receive written confirmation of the arrangements. Some speakers seem unaware of the exigencies of printed programmes and many a Programme Secretary, desperate at the nearness of her deadline, has rung up a speaker to find she was expecting to send her answer much nearer the time of the talk itself. Finally, promise to give a reminder just before the date of the meeting.

As soon as you get her confirmation of the arrangement, ink the name and title of the talk into that space of the diary. Then, about a week before the talk, write or preferably phone the speaker. The reminder is quite essential. Speakers do sometimes forget, they lose their diaries, move away, go to hospital or even die. In any case, you need up-to-date transport information.

Just occasionally the precaution is all too justified; the speaker cannot fulfil her engagements. Don't panic but welcome a rare opportunity. Consult the special list (which you will have been unobtrusively compiling) of people who have a tale to tell but for one reason or another would not fit comfortably into a pre-planned printed programme. They may live too erratic a life to risk any engagement more than a couple of days ahead or may be such worriers that, though doing perfectly well if not given time to get worked up, they cannot stand the stress of delay; there may even be some who have lived rather near the fringes of acceptability. After all, 'My years as an undetected spy' might attract quite the wrong kind of audience but as an emergency replacement the talk might well be enthralling.

Unscheduled talks almost always go down very well indeed, sometimes simply because a situation has been saved but surprisingly often on sheer merit. Nevertheless, resist all entreaties for a repetition. Second hearings are invariably disappointing.

Preparing for print
As soon as the diary is fairly complete, start to work out the display on paper. An earlier programme is the best guide to layout but the surprise of an occasional change is often stimulating and may provoke rewarding suggestions. Be sure that the shape and size you plan for the printed programme will fit a modern standard envelope then find a sheet of paper more or less the same shape but larger. Type out every capital letter, all columns and each piece of narrative. Draw the whole outline of any box enclosing special announcements so that all details show up clearly, giving no room for doubt. Make sure every item of punctu-

ation you need is undeniably there but cut out as much of this as you can if you want to stay friends with your printer. Decide whether you want the margins to be in straight lines vertically (that is, 'justified'). In print, as in type, this is easy at the left side. To produce a justified right margin is less easy in type or in loose print, so discuss this with the printer, and also ask which founts (styles of lettering) of print are available for each part of your layout. There is much greater choice in actual print than on a typewriter. Finally and at every stage, re-check all dates. Mistakes causing endless confusion are all too easily made. Finally, at this stage, while waiting for the proofs, get the envelopes addressed, ready for distribution to members.

Proofs

Even for cards, these will be on paper and if both surfaces are to be printed, the sheets will probably be clipped back to back to simulate double-sided card. Only if the print is really badly out of alignment is comment warranted for until proofs are passed, the block of print is less likely to be firmly fixed than tied rather loosely together.

Proof reading is a job not be rushed. It needs two people, one reading from the original, one from the proof, then again with reversed roles. Printing inconsistencies are more likely to be noticed by someone who had no hand in the compilation; factual errors are more obvious to the arranger. Mark the proof lightly to indicate each mistake but make separate notes of the corrections needed. Avoid proof-readers' symbols unless you have been trained in their use. Just occasionally an entire line goes missing so start by reading straight through for general sense then again check all dates and numbers. Make sure that any exceptions to standard programme arrangements are really eye-catching. People get annoyed if they turn up at the normal time to find the meeting changed. Look for incorrect letters or symbols (for 'literals' as they are called). Printers' errors are corrected free; correction of your mistakes might be charged for.

Check for consistency of symbols. The accepted use of full stops or upper case (that is, capital) letters changes from time to time and styles which may each be acceptable look sloppy if mixed. You can easily miss inconsistencies when reading straight through, so check each symbol in turn right through the programme. For example, a full stop between letters (e.g. or eg, AGM or A.G.M.) is not important in itself but the same convention should be maintained throughout.

If you have to put something in parenthesis, remember that if the sentence started inside the bracket its full stop must also be within that bracket. If the bracket is part of a sentence which has already started, its full stop will come somewhere after the second bracket. Meanwhile, consult your printer as to colour of ink and card. The available choice is never wide, and may vary from time to time, so unless your card is the same from one year to another, try to get a combination which is easy to pick out from others and also easy to read.

Finally, tot up the minimum number of cards needed, allowing at least one for every actual and prospective member, each speaker on that programme and the next, each local newspaper and advertising point (some of which seem to lose their cards as fast as they get them, but they do matter, so prepare to be generous). The total suggested number may startle a new Hon Treasurer but a second printing might cost as much as the first, whereas a large printrun costs little more than a small one. Programme cards are excellent advertisements, they cost little to store and often prove their value when historical displays are planned and on many other unforeseen occasions. A good stock rarely comes amiss in the long run.

On the day of the meeting

Start your preparations when choosing your footwear! Obvious tiptoeing movements or clicking heels irritate everyone, so unless the meeting room is carpeted, make sure your heels are silent. If you have given this reminder to anyone who might also have to move about during the speeches, the meeting should go that much more smoothly.

Be at the meeting room early so as to get everything ready before most members arrive, and certainly before the speaker does, whether or not she is bringing equipment. While others are getting ready for the meeting in their own ways, you should concentrate on the needs of the platform or dais or wherever the speaker will be stationed. Check that absolutely everything asked for is in place and working, plugged in and tested, projectors focussed and their tilt corrected, blackouts fixed or fixable without fuss and someone available who understands and can work the equipment. If slides or wallcharts are to be shown make sure a pointer is conspicuously available.

On a convenient tray arrange glasses and a carafe or jug of freshly drawn water but do not pour from it. Some speakers value the opportunity to hesitate, ostensibly to pour water though actually to collect thoughts. Unless a tap is nearby, have more than one glass on the tray in case of a persistent cougher in the audience.

If a speaker has asked for it, put a lectern with functional reading light conveniently placed to illuminate a script but do not offer these. It is no compliment to anyone to imply that she does not speak '*extempore*' (pronounced *eks-TEM-por-ay*, from the phrase meaning 'out of time'). This word has changed its implied meaning, and now has the sense of 'off the cuff' or spontaneously. It originally indicated an apology for the small amount of time which had been available to devote to written composition, but it is now recognised as demonstrating the more difficult and usually more worthwhile skill of speaking with little or no written support.

Even when slides are to be shown, encourage your speaker to remain at the front, facing her audience. It may be illogical but people do hear much better when they can see the speaker's face, even by dull reflected light, and they feel subconsciously bereft if the speaker stays by the projector, out of sight of the audience.

If the table at your disposal is just basic, try to find a tablecloth long enough to reach the floor in front. This is often termed a 'modesty-shield' for it hides the rather unbeautiful view sometimes presented by seated women wearing short straight skirts!

If the press are expected, place their table sideways to and in front of the main table or just below the platform so that everyone can see and those who should be seen, can be. If there is to be any kind of presentation, hide the object close by and easily available, however disguised.

See that the Chair's gong, gavel or bell is on the table and also her notes. On these you will have written, in addition to any special or topical notices, the exact title of the talk as printed in the programme, the speaker's title, name and qualifications, etc. Leave a space for Chair to add her own notes. Then, below the gap, write down who is to thank the speaker or (in old-fashioned terminology), Propose the Vote of Thanks. Write this formally for in moments of stress even the most familiar name can slip a memory. Don't put anything on the paper which should not be read out.

Make sure of three people in the audience, prepared to do important jobs, suitably seated if possible. A slightly deaf member can help everyone by sitting toward the back and being prepared to call out if the speaker's voice is not carrying. Someone who, if no genuine question is immediately forthcoming, will guarantee to ask something is a real comfort. She, too, is best placed toward the back to make sure the discussion stays general rather than becoming a quiet conversation around the speaker, for if that starts, members will chat among themselves. Whoever has agreed to thank the speaker should if possible sit against a wall so that when she is on her feet no listener is behind her.

Finally, check that the relevant loo is above reproach.

Starting and ending the meeting

A convenient time before she is due station yourself where you can see and be seen by an approaching speaker. Greet her. Take her to the meeting room. Make sure of the safety of her possessions. Help her unpack and fit up any equipment she has brought. Indicate the appropriate lavatory. If there is a suitable moment, introduce her to the Chair but (as Chair probably has other duties) soon reclaim the speaker and prepare to answer her questions about audience, group, lecture room and whatever else catches her interest, for often a speaker likes to bring in topical or local references.

If the speaker arrives before or during a business meeting, she will probably expect the Chair to ignore her so as not to distract the audience. She will probably prefer to sit quietly at the back, summing up the acoustics and the audience, until the close of the business part of the meeting. That is the time to take her to the front and, if it was not previously possible, introduce her to Chair. At that time much of the equipment and several of the members are likely to be in the wrong place for the next part of the activities and everyone is in the wrong mental gear for a lecture, so unless an interval for refreshments is customary, the best transition is for the Chair to announce a very short break. This gives everyone time and opportunity for physical movement (often welcomed after prolonged concentration on business), freedom to reorganise equipment and for everyone to re-seat themselves suitably.

In days gone by Chairman and speaker sat side by side so that the Chair could offer protection from a hostile audience. Nowadays, when projected slides are far commoner than hostile members, a Chair may prefer to sit in the front row of the audience, but although she may herself be more comfortable there, she cannot do her job so well. She can neither see if there is trouble of any kind in the hall nor pass a note to a speaker who is over-running her time. However, by sitting sideways-on to the audience, level with and facing the speaker, she will be able (with a little neck-craning) to see the slides and also the whole of the hall. The speaker also should feel more relaxed if able to see whether signals are being sent or the passing of time is causing anxiety. From this position Chair can deal with questions whether put in the traditional form of 'Mme Chair, may I ask whether the speaker considers that . . .?' (to which she usually responds by simply looking toward the speaker who gives the answer direct) or as is now more usual, she can leave the speaker to take full charge yet herself be ready to translate a question put in rather broad local dialect or repeat for the benefit of members with imperfect hearing questions put in gentle voices.

When questions become less pressing or 'locking-up' time is near, and whichever way Chair has been facing, she stands up, looking toward the members. If she does this with conviction all audiences recognise the signal and only rarely will a persistent questionner get in the last word. Soon, all will be silent, waiting for Chair to thank the speaker.

Thanks

Sometimes Chair, only, thanks the speaker, but as that can seem rather perfunctory, it is usual for the main thanks to come from the floor, bringing someone else into the limelight for a few moments.

Unfortunately, echoes of out-of-date routines still cling to this small duty, making modest people reluctant to perform it, unconsciously transgressing the universal rule of good manners which says that all should be prepared to 'Say Thank You Nicely' when requested! Time was when a Vote of Thanks was exactly that. In the days when learned men read their prepared papers, thankers, warned beforehand, could borrow the text and at leisure compose their own speeches, beautifully expressed, totally relevant and even including quotations.

Starting 'Mr Chairman, I rise to propose that a Vote of Thanks be conveyed from this meeting to Prof Smith for the learned paper he has just read to the Society . . .' it ended with '. . . I beg to move this proposition'. The Motion would be formally and briefly seconded from the floor then put to the meeting by the Chairman who ended with '. . . and I ask you to show this in the usual way', setting the example by starting to clap.

Nowadays things are different. When lecturers speak from minimum notes, if any, no-one can tell before the talk what will be said. Thanks composed beforehand might welcome the speaker's approval of an attitude which in fact she condemned, or refer to a subject not mentioned in the talk. A short, *extempore* speech, however expressed, does at least deal with the lecture actually given, so it is safest (unless the order of speaking has to be printed) to wait until the day then ask someone already in the lecture room to speak on behalf of the members. The extra responsibility may somewhat mar the thanker's carefree enjoyment of that particular meeting, but it is small enough return for the carefree enjoyment of so many other meetings. Whatever her feelings, when approached she should answer something on the lines of 'I don't really want to but it would be selfish and rude of me to refuse. Yes, I'll do my best'.

The usual modern routine at the end of question time is for the Chair to express her own thanks in a couple of informal sentences at most, ending '. . . but I will ask Mrs Norris to speak for us all'. Mrs Norris, if wise, will steer clear of the formal phrases of the speechwriter. She might, on getting to her feet, say 'Well, wasn't that fun . . .' or, on a different note, 'Yes, Mme Chair, I'm glad to have the privilege of thanking . . .' then concentrate on giving, in at most two minutes, a convincing impression that she really did enjoy the talk, taking up just a couple of relevant points (how vivid the anecdotes, how clear the articulation) and, if the speaker brought helpers, thanking them, too. She should try not to be fulsome and certainly should not choose that moment to ask a question for it would have to be answered and the whole routine would be disrupted.

She will probably end by turning to the speaker and saying, emphatically, 'THANK YOU, Miss Crawford' and sitting down.

The audience should, without prompting, start to clap, Mrs Norris joining in, for it is the original speech, not hers, which is being applauded. When the applause starts to wane, but not before, the Chair makes the next move, giving out notices, if any, or directing everyone toward coffee.

After the talk
You must, of course, make sure that the Hon Treasurer has handed over a sufficient cheque but the visitor's eventual memories of the group will depend less on the cheque than on your members' attitudes. Nothing warms a speaker's heart more than a queue of people anxious to continue a discussion or put yet another question; few things chill it more than being left with no-one taking any further interest, so at all times encourage your members to display (or, if necessary, simulate) continued interest in the speaker and her subject. And do see that people give more than a passing glance at her illustrative material. If this includes articles for sale she will have warned you so that you could organisae a special table with a reliable member in attendance and a float of cash available.

Try to develop a routine by which, when the departure of the speaker is imminent, one or two people will make it their business to help you collect her goods and take them towards her car or train, making sure she has not left anything behind. Other members, though by then justifiably busy about their own affairs, should be alert to pause and chorus their farewells and renewed thanks.

If numbers have been disappointing, which usually implies that your choice of speaker or subject was unwise, you might at sometime make a passing reference perhaps to some unforeseen local happening, but then let the subject slide. Repetition simply draws attention to the lack of support.

Later

Prepare to write a final note of appreciation to the speaker. True, it is a work of supererogation but it gives pleasure out of all proportion to the time taken and the cost of the stamp. If the speaker comes from a district not covered by the group's local paper and there is any expectation that the talk will be favourably reported, postpone writing then enclose the dated cutting, as a contribution to the speaker's own Cuttings Book.

Press, Promotion and Publicity Secretary

This job, fairly easily separated from that of Hon Secretary, is likely to suit someone who appreciates words, attends most meetings and enjoys working alone or with one other person to compare nuances of meaning.

Routine reports

Though you will at first find it exhilarating to see your own efforts, however humble, in real print, deflation is apt to follow when you first realise that your words have not carried quite the meaning you intended. The same thing has happened at some time to all reporters, professional as well as amateur. And always remember that your wording may be changed (and sometimes for the better) though you can't complain if its meaning suffers.

Published reports are, to all intents and purposes, advertisements. Your job is to make sure the public image of the group is as true a one as possible and at least as stimulating. Make sure the press know how to get hold of you by sending with every communication a covering letter on the group's notepaper, giving your own status as Press Officer and your name, address and phone number. Then, if the Editor notices anything in the report worth following up, or is curious about anything not in the report, there should be no difficulty in making contact.

When you are first appointed, ring up your local papers and ask about deadlines (that is, the last moments when copy received has a chance of appearing in the next issue). Whatever the timing or the content, there is no guarantee that it will get in (as an Editor has said 'if there's a double murder in the High Street, I doubt if we'll have time or space for you'!) but if it has not appeared in the next issue, give up expecting it; it will no longer be news.

Find out how long your reports should be by counting the words of the printed equivalents from other groups. You can be sure that if yours is too long it will be cut and the gems of phraseology you treasure most always seem the first to go. You'll best succeed in your hope of catching the eye of the casual reader if you entirely cut out all reference to routine matters for they are, frankly, dull to outsiders. Start with a stimulating incident, phrase or idea and follow this up with other exciting activities in whatever order seems interesting, irrespective of their actual order of occurrence.

If you discover your Editor has individual quirks, pander to them by all means but be assured some rules hold for all Editors. Among the most important is the Rule of the Five W's . . . Who, Why, Where, What and When though amateur press officers of groups can usually ignore the last of these, 'At a recent meeting . . .' being more useful to the Editor who has to allot space. By contrast, 'Who' is always important. Editors love names — initials, forenames, surnames, titles, hyphens — and all must be absolutely accurate.

Most editors are wary of the higher flights of literacy. Verse, however *apropos* and well-known, will almost certainly be cut out. If acronyms or sets of initials are used, they should be written in full on their first appearance for, as the Dictionary of Initials has shown, most sets have several meanings. And, above all, remember that an editor is the only 'we' in the newspaper world.

Having composed your report, type it, however beautiful your handwriting. Use double or triple spacing and wide margins on one side of the paper only. Keep in your own file a dated carbon copy of everything you send in.

After a while, compare these originals with the printed version being saved for the Scrap Book. Any differences may teach salutary lessons.

Staff reporters

Staff reporters, from the paper's full-time staff, occasionally appear at a group's open events simply because the activities seemed interesting (quite the best kind of publicity for anyone with a clear conscience) or perhaps because the Mayor or Mayoress has decided to attend. Usually it is because you or your Committee felt that the event warranted a professional write-up and sent a complimentary ticket to the paper. Such invitations are rarely acknowledged for reporters can never guarantee not to be sent to some other assignment, especially in the evenings, when fewer of them are on duty. You and your Committee must balance the cost of a dinner which will have to be paid for, eaten or not, against a professional write-up, which would appear in the main columns of the newspaper but which simply might not eventuate or could just miss the essence of the event, whereas you would have stressed it. If a reporter is present you are never off duty.

Reporters expect to be taken to all special guests and to have names and dates supplied accurately and answers given to all their relevant questions. Remember that they must pick up what stories they can where they can. If you leave them free to meet all and sundry they might discover among the other guests a more interesting story than yours!

Press photographers

Catastrophes apart, most papers print no photos other than their own, so if you consider that a coming event warrants a published picture, ring up your local reporters' room a couple of weeks beforehand. Whoever answers, give your name and that of your group with, if necessary, some reminder of its recent published activities. Briefly describe the planned event and the important local and visiting people you expect at it, asking for a photographer and/or reporter to attend. The date will be noted in their Diary; you will be asked to phone a reminder a couple of days before the event but there will be no promises to attend. However, you can be fairly sure someone will turn up for a handing over of a charity cheque, the passing on of Presidential insignia or the like, if only because these events can be easily re-staged.

Let the meeting itself be run on the assumption that no press will arrive, then, if a photographer does appear, stop everything else and stage the presentation, even if it has actually taken place or is not yet due. There will probably be snaps of a surprisingly large number of slightly different versions. Unless you are lucky, all will show everyone standing awkwardly in a line, grinning toward the camera. The photographer will note down essential details of names, etc, and if no reporter is likely to be there as well (and the liaison between newspaper staff is always good) the photographer will take down at least enough information to compose an extended caption. You should be on hand throughout, for it is up to you to supply, accurately, any further details needed. You might like to prepare a short report, typed and absolutely accurate, ready to hand over. It may save time and will possibly help get some detail included which would otherwise be missed.

Poster advertising
Poster advertising is a quite different aspect of your job, and very important for special occasions.

Posters must necessarily be eye-catching so use as little lettering as possible. What words there are should have thick enough lines to be legible from a distance. Except where theatrical traditions still hold, A4 is the largest paper most shops will display. A5 is convenient for hand-outs and enclosures. Each should include at least the name of the group and its logo, if any; the title of the event and its type (lecture, drama, outing, match); where it will take place; when it will take place, date and time; price to members and to visitors; and an eye-catching illustration if it seems appropriate.

Broadcasting
If your group gets the opportunity to broadcast, take it unhesitatingly. It may be that your Chair, however well she functions as Chair, is not a fluent speaker. Never mind. Do not emphasise protocol. Everyone will be happier if the group can be represented by a fluent, knowledgeable speaker even if she comes from 'the floor', not even from the Committee.

Links with other groups
The more successful your publicity, the more likely people are to want to get in touch with your group. Many places have a kind of local Directory of Official and Voluntary Organisations, listing aims, names and contact phone numbers. Someone, probably you, ought to check that your group's details are kept up-to-date and accurate. Make sure that the details are independently available at all recognised information points in your area, including Library, Museum, CAB and Tourist Information centres.

HONORARY TREASURER

An Hon Treasurer must, above all, feel comfortable with money for she is ultimately responsible for every financial transaction undertaken by the group, whether getting, spending or saving, and for recording these transactions. Her books will have none of the complexities of 'double entry' accounting which, being designed for recording business profits or losses, has no place among the activities of amateur, non-profit-making groups.

The job has more to it than just adding up a column of figures (and not absconding with the funds!) but almost any numerate person, however inexperienced, should be able to follow my instructions. Unlike Secretaries, Treasurers all do much the same job and the routine for recording the basics has become so nearly universal that it can be given in fair detail. Let's start the description of the whole financial cycle at the close of the AGM when you take over and when subscriptions, newly-fixed, first become due.

Subscriptions
Subscriptions are primarily tokens of membership showing acceptance of the group's Rules and linked with voting rights; their level is usually governed by expenditure. They used not to change for years on end but inflation led to the administrative nuisance of frequent rises and as every rise gives waverers an excuse to resign, the necessary increases now tend to be occasional but large.

No subscriptions are likely to be acceptable until the AGM when the previous year's members determine the level for the current year. Most groups expect running costs to be covered by the subscription, every member bearing some share of them, but some prefer to set dues at a lower level, then make an additional charge at each meeting, often by a high price for the usual hot drink, so that costs fall most heavily on those who attend most often. A few, by calling on other sources of revenue such as jumble sales or donations, keep subscriptions down to mere tokens so that no-one need feel excluded, but, generally, not many join who would not have done so at economic levels.

In many sets of Rules the item governing subscriptions includes wording such as 'anyone who (having been individually reminded) has not paid her subscription by . . . (the crossing off date) will be deemed lapsed, though full payment will ensure full re-instatement'. The arrangement is totally beneficial. The group does not need to send circulars to people who thought they had left it; members relax, knowing that if they forget to pay they will be personally reminded, and you, as Treasurer, by administering the rule efficiently and tactfully will free yourself from several potential loose ends.

Membership list
Do always remember to give the Hon Secretary the name of all who have been crossed off as well as all who have joined, re-joined, resigned, moved or died, for though yours is the definitive membership list, hers probably gets more use and mistakes in it can as easily upset the members.

While you are about it, why not make one of the lists, or files, really informative by including references to members' talents and interests. Long before the data may be needed for a really appreciative obituary, they will have been consulted by officers, especially those new to the area and its inhabitants, needing to find suitable people to meet interested visitors. But beware of ever writing anything even verging on the libellous.

Dealing with cash
When doing this, never let yourself be rushed or flurried.

At the end of the AGM put a comfortable chair in a convenient place and sort out your requirements – pens, a counted float of change (to keep the group's money separate from yours), a clip to hold cheques and banknotes, the group's rubber stamp if receipts are not 'personalised' and the current receipt book. Its pages should have consecutive printed numbers, be perforated for easy detachment and stamped or printed with the group's logo so that the members can easily identify them later. It will have stubs or, better, be interleaved with duplicates so that you will have a written carbon record of every transaction. As each payment is made, fill in the date, the payer's name, the amount she has paid and its purpose, probably here, 'Subscription'. Sign it and hand it over, asking the member, as she now is, to check that all is correct. Keep the duplicates safely. At the end of the financial year they will be wanted again. Before you go home count your 'takings' and bag the money, keeping it separate from any other.

On getting home, check that you have received all the books and papers listed as the Treasurer's responsibility then turn again to your immediate business. Check the sum of cash and cheques brought from the meeting against the totals in the receipt book for that day. If the two figures do not tally, find the reason and make the necessary corrections. As soon as possible, pay the money, preferably as a single unit, into the bank.

Banks

Banks will always accept money, even from strangers, but will only pay it out or move it from one account to another on the authority of a recognised signature; if the money is held in trust, as group funds are, banks require at least two signatures (and Treasurers will expect this safeguard for the group's funds). To get signatures recognised, go to the group's bank and ask for the relevant form. It will have spaces for recording the sample signatures of at least four people, those continuing from the previous year being guarantee for the new ones. To allow for holidays and broken arms, always record more signatures than you expect to need. If your group's use of that bank is new, offer a copy of your Rules to the person who deals with the group's affairs.

Keep a very small store of cheques ready signed by one of the other recognised officers. When you need to make a payment by cheque, countersign it only just before posting or handing it over to the payee. If you plan to be away for a time you can reverse this process without risk to the group's savings by putting your signature on enough blank cheques to tide them over, leaving the other officer to countersign at the last moment.

Recording income

Treasurers are expected to be able to say, almost whenever asked, just how well their group is doing financially. With the accumulation of stubs, receipts etc, you would find this increasingly difficult but for a helpful and almost universal routine. By summarising everything as you go along in one single Book of Account you can see how things are, almost at a glance. Then, at the year-end, you can boil down the same data still further to give a clear, one-page summary or Statement. Even if you were quite new to the job, members would normally trust your Statement for always a qualified outsider, called an Auditor, is engaged to test the accuracy of your figures by comparing the duplicates, stubs, vouchers, etc, against your entries in your Books of Account. The drill for making the entries is surprisingly simple. Let's go through it stage by stage.

A purpose-printed book makes recording easier but in small new groups an ordinary exercise book would do and is probably best if you and your group are having to learn from the beginning. Start by writing up in pencil in case at first you get into temporary muddles, then ink in the figures when you are reasonably sure they are correct.

Soon, whether in an exercise book or a printed ledger, you should be making all entries in ink and never permitting an erasure. If you do make a mistake, cross it out and write the correct figure nearby, in ink. In due course you should progress to a well-bound book with numbered pages and purpose-printed rulings, each space being just the size for one single entry, leaving no room for unauthorised additions. Every transaction should be written up as soon as possible so it is high time to start recording the subscriptions you took at the AGM.

Open the ledger at the first available double spread for that, not the page, is the unit which will show simultaneously 'getting' and 'spending'. Prepare to record 'getting' (ie Income (or Receipts)) on the left-hand page, called the verso and 'spending' (Payments), on the right, the recto. Near the left-hand edge above the top line of the verso write the Year. If you are using an exercise book you will need to rule vertical columns where I describe those of the printed ledger, experimenting to find how narrow each can be. Write into Column 1, on the left, the rest of the date in your favoured shortened notation. Let's say the AGM was on February 3rd or, perhaps '3.ii' or '3/2/ '. In Column 2, rather wide, pack in on one line a description of the transaction, this time the taking of (say) ten subscriptions '10 subs'. In the space in Column 3, write the numbers printed on the receipts, (say 37−46). These will tell you who paid and that all paid the full subscription (say £3.00). In the space above Column 4 write the word 'total' and in that column, in the line you have started, write the total amount you received (ie £30.00). The rest of the line is set off into columns which will eventually represent the group's main sources of income. One source is sure to be subscriptions so put that heading above the first column of this dissected part of the page. As you find you need, or by copying from earlier pages, head most of the other columns with other sources of income, including, don't forget, 'Miscellaneous'. In the 'Subscriptions' column write £30.00, an apparent duplication which you will soon see is actually a guard against mistakes. You have finished with that line until that page is filled.

Let's move on to the next money you receive, possibly at the next monthly meeting. Again ten people pay subscriptions but one of them in a hurry, generous and with nothing smaller than a £5.00 note, says 'Put the change into the funds'. Make out her receipt for what she has paid and what she has paid for, ie '£5.00 for sub and donation'. Write out the summary in your ledger much as last time but this time it will start '3.iii. 10 subs etc, 47−56. £32'. This in itself is incomplete. Head the next free column 'Donations' and in this column write '£2.00'. Now you see why there is a 'totals' column which will have an entry on every line and also other, dissected, columns, not used on every line but with entries which will together tally with the totals column.

Recording expenditure

Record payments in much the same way. Make the payment by cheque if possible so that you have a permanent record. Enter the information on the other page, the recto. Almost the only difference will be that on this page it is cheque numbers not receipt numbers which you write into Column 3. As before, write the total in its column then enter it also in whatever column or columns of the dissected section of the page best reflect the purpose of the payment.

Checking entries on a full page

You will probably not fill verso and recto at the same rate but when either has only the bottom line unused, check both, ready for turning the page and re-starting. Add up all the dissected or sub-divided columns. Have you seen this total recently? It should, logically, be the same as the answer at the bottom on the 'totals' column. If it is not, there is a mistake somewhere which you must find and correct. Now you can ink in the whole bottom line. In the leftermost column, fill in the date and in the 'Transactions' column write 'C/fd', the recognised abbreviation for 'Carried forward'.

Turn the page and, continuing recto to recto or verso to verso, ink in the headings above the columns exactly as on the completed page; any change now would only cause confusion. The time for change is at the end of the financial year. In the top left-hand corner again write the year. In the left-hand column on the top line write the date, which should be the same as the last on the previous double spread. In the 'transactions' column write 'Bt/Fd', the recognised abbreviation of 'Brought forward', then copy in all the totals from the bottom of the filled page. Make sure that you have done this correctly by totalling the dissected column totals to make sure they still tally with the 'totals' column. That page is now ready for use. It contains a summary of the summarised transactions on the previous page which, therefore, you probably will not need even to look at until the end of the financial year.

Turn back the page. Complete the page facing the one you have just dealt with, even if this one is not full. Add the money columns and check the sub-divisions against the total exactly as for the filled page and when all is correct, ink in the bottom line, turn the page and copy the figures into the top line of the new one. However, to make sure no-one makes illicit use of the blank lines on the part-filled page (and to protect yourself from any suggestion that you invited such illicit use) rule an ink line diagonally from the bottom date in the first column to the final figure in the bottom right-hand corner.

Repeat all this throughout the year as a page in each double spread is filled. The top line of each double spread will give a summary of the group's income and expenditure (its receipts and payments) since the end of the last financial year and a glance at the figures below it should always enable you to state with reasonable accuracy just how the group stands. Continue this routine until the year-end.

Audit

Anyone who handles money other than her own should expect to be subjected to some kind of audit so this is a logical culmination of every Treasurer's need to be seen to be an accurate recorder and above suspicion; also of any group's wish to be assured that their money is in good hands. Rather than everyone trying to examine the books for herself, members share the responsibility by appointing at an AGM a non-member, skilled with figures, of known good reputation, and not closely linked with the Treasurer (minimising the suspicion of collusion which could arise when large funds are involved), to search the books and supporting papers then sign a declaration that the Statement is accurate (if, indeed it is).

Many people and firms do this professionally for a fee but in most communities there are a few suitable people, often retired, who will audit the books of small, worthwhile groups and do it free as their form of community service (they are, nevertheless, usually willing to accept the occasional book token or complimentary ticket to the group's Annual Dinner). Most communities owe a real debt to the many people who give this kind of quiet support in so many spheres, and usually with minimal thanks or recognition. Be considerate to your Auditor, whether or not she is paid. Well before the year-end, discuss with her the last date for getting the books to her which will let her go through them and still leave you time to get the audited statement reprographed for the AGM. It probably does not leave you long after the year-end to finalise the Statement.

Try to collect all money owed to the group before the crucial day and take care to pay all bills. Your aim is to be absolutely neutral on that night, neither owing nor owed one penny. Your task will be that much easier if you always bear in mind that the date of the end of the Financial Year was chosen as being the time when your group's financial activity would be at its lowest. When the programme is under consideration try to ensure that each event is timed so that any money due from it can come in and all relevant bills be paid out during the same financial year. You will then be able to give the Auditor, and the AGM, a completed, not an interim, account of every event.

Year-end Statement

This one-page summary must include, all boiled down together, every financial transaction the group has taken part in during the year and show clearly whether the result was a gain or a loss. Money isn't everything but if their group's savings are draining away, members will want to know why, so try to make the statement as complete and as self-explanatory as possible. Always take all your books to the AGM ready to quote details in support of your Statement.

Petty cash books

Officers, and sometimes others, need to hold a small amount of cash to spend on behalf of the group, recording it in a 'petty cash notebook'. Each sum you hand over should be recorded twice, by you on the recto of your cash book as an outgoing, by her on the verso of her petty cash book as income for her office. Each time she spends any of the money she makes a note of it on the outgoings (recto) page of her book, even if it is to pay herself for the use, on behalf of the group, of her private phone. As you top up her money supply or as she spends it, each sum is entered appropriately.

As the end of the Financial Year approaches, remind her of this, then on the last evening she should total both what she has received and what she has spent and by subtracting one from the other find what the balance should be and make quite sure it is accounted for by the money and stamps in her cashbox. You will need to know all three figures, her income (which should agree with your records) and her outgoings and the balance she still has in hand.

A few people may have an 'imprest'. This is the basis for a minor form of trading as when the catering officer buys milk, biscuits and tea and then makes a small profit by selling very light refreshments to the members. The money might be handed over after each meeting or only at the year-end, but either way all sums should be entered as gross figures, not net, that is, showing both costs and takings, not just profits.

Remember to ask the bank for a full statement up to and including the last day of the year. The deposit statement will include all the interest which has accrued to the account and which you will record as part of the group's income. Total and check all columns in the final double spread of your ledger even if only part of each page has been used. These figures summarise the entire year's income on one page and expenditure on the other. They will be the basis of your statement. Make sure no more entries can be made on those pages by drawing diagonal lines across the unused part of each. The figures next year will be entered overleaf and the columns may have different headings. You are ready to start compiling your Statement.

Income and Expenditure Account

This, sometimes called the Receipts and Payments Account, is a summary of all the items recorded in your ledger for the year, the two lists arranged to indicate your group's main interests and to show which had been the greater during that year, income or expenditure.

Start with whichever side of the ledger you prefer. On spare paper arrange, column-wise and labelled, all the dissected totals from the bottom of the page. Check that they still add up to the figure at the bottom of column 4. Glance down the column 2 of all pages of the year to find if the headings of the dissected columns are as helpful as they might be. Would they be more vivid if some items with a natural affinity, such as Telephone, Postages and Printing, were amalgamated, even if they must first be sorted out from other totals such as the petty cash book? Don't worry if the number of items changes provided the money total does not.

Do the same for the other page. Some items might be closely related to one already on the page and totalled, for example, perhaps the proceeds of a sale and the costs of running that sale. Highlight any such relationships in your Statement, perhaps by keeping the related items at the same level when the two lists are printed side by side so that members' eyes sweep across from one to the other eg:

Subs . . . .£300.00   Capitation Fees £240.00

Alternatively, you could put small subtraction sums in the narrative, eg:

Subs £300.00
Less capitation fee .£240.00
                      £60.00

Try to arrange most items in descending order of their interest to your group; in money-raising groups gifts to charity would probably be top of the list but be much lower down in pressure groups.

Write the two columns side by side, leaving a blank space below both final figures. Find the total of each column and note it on rough paper. Write the larger of the totals under both blank spaces. Now one column does not add up correctly. Make it do so by writing the difference between the totals in the appropriate blank space. Let it stand out stark and clear. It is the first figure your members will look for. It represents either the Excess of Income over Expenditure or Excess of Expenditure over Income. Label it appropriately.

Your Auditor, even if she agreed with your totals, might possibly be puzzled by your amalgamations or arrangements and suggest a discussion. Be grateful for an excellent chance to seek advice. Some auditors go further in dealing with inexperienced amateur Treasurers and are willing to compile the Statements as well as checking that the income and expenditure were as shown in the totals. That account would, of course, be accurate but the amalgamations might not truly reflect that group's balance of activities. If such an offer is made, take it up gladly but on condition that it becomes a joint enterprise so that you can learn more about compiling a statement and can describe in greater detail your group's interests.

This Statement will tell everyone how well you have managed over the year and is normally titled the 'Income and Expenditure Account for the Financial Year . . . to . . .'. If, occasionally, Rules have to be changed so that the dates of the Financial Year are altered, change the title of the Statement. Head it '. . . for the PERIOD starting . . . and ending . . .'. Do not lightly change your Financial Year, for it prevents year by year comparison.

Completing the financial picture

Normally, this account will deal with the financial activity during precisely one year, the financial year recently finished. But what about the savings from previous years? What about that money waiting unspent in cashboxes and accounts? All that still needs to be accounted for.

Add together all the money in hand at the ending of the financial year with the origin of each sum, that is, which cashbox or which bank account. Add them together. This is the nest egg you handed over to the future on the last night of the financial year. Write down those figures and their total as a payment — a payment to the future.

Unless your group is less than a year old, you should be remembering that at the start of the financial year you are dealing with, you took over quite a lot of money, cash in the boxes of some officers, and also probably some bank

HERE AND THERE SOCIETY
Income and Expenditure Account
for year 1 Aug 1980 – 31 July 1981

Aug'79 Jul'80	RECEIPTS				Aug'79 Jul'80	PAYMENTS	
116	Subscriptions 62 at £3	186.00			40	Speaker's Expenses	131.50
	1 at £1.50	1.50	187.50		17	Rent of Lecture Room	73.00
2	Visitors		16.00		14	Printing etc,	27.41
–	Donations		106.66		14	Secretary's Expenses	32.75
–	Sale of unwanted chairs	35.00			1	Treasurer's Expenses	0.60
	less carriage	5.00	30.00		–	Bank Charges	0.93
–	Sponsorship Local Council		10.00		39	EXCESS OF RECEIPTS OVER PAYMENTS	122.93
(6)	Visits Takings	15.00					
	Less costs	5.00	10.00				
4	Coffees Takings	7.60					
	Less costs	2.10	5.50				
9	Interest on deposit account		23.46				
125			389.12		125		389.12

OPENING BALANCES 1st August 1980

Deposit Account		113.48
Current Acount		67.17
Total cash in hand		8.40
ADD Excess of receipts over payments during current year		122.93
		311.98

CLOSING BALANCES 31st July 1981

Deposit Account		253.94
Current Account		36.51
Cash in hand	Sec 4.78	
	Treas 5.98	
	Refresh Sec 1.64	
	Visits Sec 9.13	21.53
		311.98

accounts. Together they form the nest egg you inherited and must be set against what you now have in hand, so make a little sum to show it. You can find the details in last year's Statement where these figures appear as being handed over to this financial year. Then they were headed 'Closing Balances'. Write them down now as the Opening Balances of this year as:

Opening Balances		Closing Balances	
Deposit Account	....	Deposit Account	....
Cheque Account	....	Cheque Account	....
Cash in hand		Cash in hand	
Chair	....	Chair	....
Sec	....	Sec	....
Treas	....	Treas	....

You now have two separate pictures. You know what you did financially during the year and also you know what you had at the start and what you had at the end of the year. Bring them together with the Balances. If you made a profit on the year, write that in the Closing Balances column. If a loss, write it on the Opening Balances side. Add up each side. They should give the same answer because what you took over from the past plus what you made during the year (or minus what you lost during the year) should equal what you were able to pass on to your successors. This final figure is called (accurately but somewhat pompously for a small group) the Accumulated Reserves. They include every penny possessed by the group on the last night of the financial year, the Income and Expenditure Account having shown how well the group had done over the year itself.

You can make this account still more meaningful to your members. They always want to know (don't we all?) whether they are doing better or worse than last year. To introduce the year-by-year comparisons into this Statement, write beside each item the equivalent figure for the previous year, taken from that Statement and Balance Sheet. Set the figures rounded down (that is, pence omitted); using a hyphen rather than leaving a blank if ever an item appears in one year but not the other, and enclose negative sums (ie debts) in brackets instead of the earlier practice of using the vivid ink which gave rise to the phrase 'being in the red'.

Meanwhile, although the group's AGM is normally held during the period of minimal activity, some bills and possibly some payments may come in. Whether or not the official books are available, do not expect to make any entries at all in them until after the AGM, if only because you must always allow for the possibility that another Treasurer may be appointed and have different ideas about the heading of the columns in the main books. During this awkward period keep specially careful notes preferably in a notebook earmarked for that job and annually brought into use.

Material assets

The group's cash may have been checked to the last penny but wealth does not consist of money alone. Many groups have material possessions bought with members' money and often with resale value above any of the sums shown in the Statement. Reassured annually of the safety of their money, members should be reassured about their material possessions as well.

Branches often show a small-scale example of this need. When badges are bought from HQ the cost is recorded as a payment and when some are sold the money for them is recorded as income. But what about any badges remaining unsold across the year-end? They, too, should appear somewhere in the record. A footnote in the Statement is probably the best solution to this problem, with the badges themselves produced as evidence.

Purchases not for resale but for use would also be recorded as an expenditure but after one entry this disappears from the accounts. When the article, perhaps a typewriter, is in constant use in a member's home, its true ownership is easily forgotten by everyone so that should be recorded somewhere, preferably in an Inventory kept among the Treasurer's official papers. The date of the purchase would be stated as part of the note, the date being the one recorded in cashbook or cheque stub. If it was a donation, give when the gift was Minuted. When, eventually, the machine is disposed of, for however small or large a sum, cross it out of the inventory, justifying the change by a note beside it of the date of the sale as recorded in the receipts page of the cash book. If monetarily worthless, it is interesting enough to be donated to some museum, make the cross-reference to the date the gift was Minuted or to the letter of thanks. If totally without scrap value, give the date of the Minute authorising its disposal to pre-empt any suggestion of wrongful removal of the group's possessions.

As with money, things should be checked annually, probably with another officer acting as your Auditor and physically handling each item. Some groups have never kept such an Inventory. If yours is one, the sooner you start the better, and you may find, when some forgotten possession is revealed as a result of your enquiries, that the group is richer than anyone thought. Unless the list was established at the foundation of the group itself, memories must be searched, Minutes and Account Books studied and the contents of desks and cupboards of long-standing members combed through. Further discoveries are never impossible, even in jumble sales or second-hand book shops.

Used Account and Minute Books are of little financial value though money was spent in buying them, but when filled, they are historically irreplaceable. List them by appearance (thick, green) and function (Minutes 1944–60) and pack together all but the current ones, lodge them in some safe place such as a bank and see that the guardianship of the receipt is Minuted. It will probably become one of the Treasurer's papers.

Distress Fund, Benevolent Fund, President's Fund, etc

Whatever name it is given, many of the groups which have use for this type of fund, always started and maintained by donations, usually keep it independent of the Financial Statement so that sometimes even the Auditor does not know of its existence and you might have no hand in its administration. It only gets enough publicity to keep it topped up and though in practice you are usually consulted, the fund is often the personal responsibility of one named officer; the incumbent officer administering it and passing its assets to her successor. This relative absence of publicity is deliberate so that members who seek its help can be confident that their problems will not become generally known, whether the fund could only just help pay a subscription or might help re-roof the family mansion.

Keeping members informed

Your members will know that money comes in and money goes out but they may not understand the whole picture without your help. It is up to you to explain, meeting by meeting, everything concerned with the group's finances, starting with a simple outline. Usually there is a rich inflow of subscriptions just after the AGM but when all members have paid no more income can be guaranteed until after the next AGM. If they want more, they must look to money-making activities or to donations.

Donations are, of course, always welcomed; your ledger will probably show several cash gifts which will all appear somewhere in your Annual Statement. But what about the gifts which do not involve cash? Many members prefer not to accept reimbursement of their own out-goings, others make no charge for doing jobs such as reprography for the group and some offer gifts in kind, such as the makings of an annual strawberry feast. These gifts are part of the group's income. Without them either standards would go down or subscriptions eventually go up, yet they cannot be passed through the Books of Account and there is no accepted routine for acknowledging them. It is up to you to find suitable ways of doing this, not necessarily naming names but expressing the group's appreciation of the gifts, having the thanks Minuted (for the benefit at least of future students of finance) and including some reference in your Annual Report.

In all this, your reporting does not just amplify a statement of figures, it replaces it. Whatever the income, expenses go relentlessly on, perhaps even with peaks as when an annual bill comes in or HQ asks for capitation fees but also, sometimes, with remissions, as in a close season for meetings when no rent has to be paid. But with income and outgoings both apt to fluctuate, members need regular written reports, preferably illuminated by the equivalent figures for the previous year. Without such information, planning for extra expenditure is risky, even for one-off expenses such as the purchase of a typewriter, much more so for a regular increase in outlay such as renting rather than borrowing a room or (especially) for employing regular paid help with its legal as well as financial obligations.

Unforeseen expenses can never be ruled out but mostly new charges are generated from inside the group and normally are within its control, not imposed from outside. This is also true of the movement of surplus funds from the cheque account to a bank deposit or other gilt-edged security which attracts interest, to add to the group's income while guaranteeing that the capital is safe. Keep to 'trustee' funds or there will be justified comments about gambling with members' money.

All this presupposes a flourishing group with at least a

sufficient and possibly a rising regular income from subscriptions, but if the impetus falters you may have to remind members that there is a limit beyond which costs cannot be cut. If you go on reporting lower balances than in the previous year with no compensating investment you should point out that when the trend is downward, donations, whether in cash or kind, (sure to be their first reaction) are of little help. Another inevitable suggestion will be that costs should be reduced by cutting out alternate meetings. The result of this is always that members forget which meetings are retained, attendance drops further and so does membership. Rather, this is the time to be enterprising. Start some new activity which will get members working together and therefore talking together. During such discussions the basic problems may be pinpointed and ideas worked out which could save the group. If money comes as well you have probably turned the corner.

Whatever the financial trend or level of the group, other activities might at any time call for your attention for you ought to take an interest in everything which even remotely or temporarily involves the group's money.

Money-making activities

I am assuming this is quite a subsidiary activity. If it is your group's main purpose, check on your rights and obligations with the National Council for Voluntary Organisations (Library and Information Unit) 26, Bedford Square, London, WC1.

Raffles
Be wary of the legal position when you organise a raffle. If outside people are involved you probably need to be registered with the police. Within small groups raffles usually go unchallenged.

If you can establish a tradition that the original donor is the only person allowed to return anything for re-drawing, guests asked to make the draw should never feel embarrassed if they pick their own number. If the winner of one raffle donates the prize for the next one, costs will be spread fairly.

Jumble sales

Jumble sales are in some ways great fun, in others a nuisance. They can make money and benefit everyone. Givers gain if they are being rid of a dust-trap, buyers gain by at last possessing, at no great cost, something perhaps long wanted. However, if you make realistic allowances for petrol consumed you may find that, even ignoring workers' time, the low pricing is difficult to justify. But does that conflict with the object of the exercise? On balance, working together and the boost to members' morale justifies most jumble sales.

Sales stalls

Their undoubted main aim is to make money for the group. Whether other considerations are even more important is for you and the Committee to decide by justifying the pricing policy to yourselves. Try working out who, at each stage, gains how much money, satisfaction, reputation, goodwill, contacts, or enjoyment and who, if anyone, loses any of these. A couple of examples may illustrate the problem.

A member, highly paid in her own job, buys ingredients and spends time sorting them in her own kitchen and making a rich fruit cake which she takes to a charity market stall where it is sold below cost.

Alternatively, a member takes a tin of peas from her own larder (replacing it when she next goes shopping) and carries it to a Bring & Buy stall. Another member, not seeing anything more attractive there, buys it at less than shop price (as is usual at Charity Stalls) and carries it all the way to her home which happens to be next door to a grocer.

Large sales

These need elaborate planning so if you embark on one, take it seriously. Make the comfort of your helpers your first consideration, taking particular care to arrange that their personal possessions — handbags, money, coats — are safe both from inadvertent sale and deliberate theft. Among other arrangements, for each stall provide a suitable float (that is, a starting supply of counted small change) to be subtracted from the final totals of stalls and of sale. Provide a cashbox for each stall or a 'money-pinny' for each helper to keep their takings safe from light fingers. Plan relays of runners with cashbags and informal receipts which they will regularly exchange at each stall and, if a charge is made for entrance, at each door for roughly counted notes and bagged coin. The runners should take these to a more secure central place for accurate counting and for safe storage. There, maintain a supply of ruled sheets for immediate, precise recording of the running totals, stall by stall, so that morale-boosting announcements of takings can be broadcast regularly. Obtain night-safe facilities and recruit enough strong men to guard the entrance and to escort takings to the bank. Inform the police of your activities.

Non-profit-making activities

Hardly anyone ever aims at making a financial loss and certainly not a Treasurer, but occasionally you may try to keep profits to the very minimum. Your group might, for example, run a reunion dinner for its retired members. If a high proportion of those eligible attended and all seemed to enjoy it, it would be considered a success. It would get even higher praise if, all bills having been paid from the ticket money, only pence, not pounds, remained. Each transaction will have been a balancing act between profit and loss, the deciding factor often being the take-up of tickets. On an inclement night there is a great deal of difference between a ticket already paid for and an invitation which, though accepted, will only be paid for when the holder gets there. At such events a prepayment rule is important and numbered tickets, listed, can be very informative.

Always beware of flattering your guests by providing costly amenities unless you are sure they will be appreciated. For example, high class music is a mistake at a reunion for people inevitably talk over it, yet you must pay live musicians their going rate, whatever their quality and whether or not anyone could hear them.

Memorials

Whether paid for from funds or by a general collection, money is almost always involved somewhere so it usually falls to you to advise on any tribute when an eminent member dies, and you would do well to make the first move. If it is the policy of your group to send flowers to a funeral you must, of course, act immediately. If she has had a long illness, surprisingly soon there will be few people left who had actually met her and in times of inflation even a generous collection soon seems pathetically trivial. As good a way as any of keeping a name alive is to buy a useful piece of equipment, fix to it a plaque with the name then habitually link that name with it, as 'Mrs Elton's projector' or 'Miss Bates' table'. If a programme is about to be published, why not link an activity with her name, especially if a spoken tribute can be included but beware of even suggesting any annual gesture, for this ties the hands of later Committees.

If a minute's silence at a meeting seems appropriate, remind Chair that this is best observed at the very start of the meeting for otherwise all may be on tenderhooks, wondering if it has been forgotten and unable to settle their possessions knowing they might have to dislodge them to stand.

Insurance of people and possessions

You, like all good Treasurers, should always be aware of the financial implications of Murphy's Law, which states that 'if something can go wrong, sooner or later it will', and it's best not to wait for the worst to happen. As you notice potential problems, put them to your Committee. Think out the details beforehand and come armed with facts, for you will be asked to give guidance, though the decision must be a group one, Minuted, and better taken before trouble arises than because trouble has arisen.

You might have to advise on people's safety. For example, if a Speaker breaks a leg while at your meeting and neither she nor the hall are insured, who pays? The HQ of some organisations arrange insurances to cover all eventualities in all branches and because the risks are so widely spread, the cost is low. Branches should ask their HQ for up-to-date details. Without this, every group, like every person, is on its own. Very occasionally, a small group has been crippled for lack of some appropriate insurance but fortunately it is a rare problem.

Insuring the group's possessions such as typewriter or insignia against theft or damage is a problem which should be considered at the same time as the first acquisition of a possession. Some insurance companies will cover a group's possessions with the other possessions of whatever officer is in temporary charge of the article, providing it has been declared on the policy but not all do this and few do it automatically.

For groups which have them, the branch's jewels or insignia are likely to be their most valuable possessions. These insignia, usually pendants which can also be worn brooch-wise, have little appeal to independent local groups. National Organisations sometimes require that each of their branches should invest in something appropriate for use at business meetings (when only the person in the chair would wear insignia) or at social events (when everyone who has such a jewel wears it). If HQ does not stipulate a standard design but leaves the group to choose its own and you are its Founder Treasurer you will be even more closely concerned, for members (at that stage mostly strangers one to another) will look to you for advice on what can be afforded, yet no-one can know what the group's income will be. There is never a 'right' answer to this problem but always bear in mind that later enhancing of something made 'on-the-cheap' is rarely successful.

If, as is customary, the pendant hangs on a ribbon, someone is sure to suggest attaching a name bar for each President as she leaves office. Members tend to find the idea attractive but you should be cautious, if only to the extent of asking who will pay for them. If the President, whether incoming or outgoing, is expected to pay, the cost might eventually deter a potentially excellent but impecunious candidate. And don't forget that if the branch flourishes, later Presidents will have to face the problem of the sheer physical weight of accumulating bars. Officers of long-established branches do complain that having to wear so much metal hanging from the neck can be almost unbearably exhausting.

Speakers' expenses

Almost every group welcomes at least an occasional lecture, so you are sure to be asked at some time for Speaker's Expenses. Smooth routine creates a good impression so work out a trouble-free way of dealing with the matter. From first making contact, direct or through the Programme Secretary, you must bear in mind the total potential cost of each event, and will probably have set an upper inclusive limit. Professional Speakers have a regular scale of charges but there is a surprising variety of possible alternatives and you will feel much happier in dealing with them if a policy has already been laid down by the Committee. Some people, whether or not they work for a charity, ask that a donation be sent in their name to some specified fund; members or local personalities who simply enjoy sharing their interest with others and do not wish to complicate their tax forms, often prefer a small token or gift. Do try to find something which can easily be carried home — not a large wired bouquet which can be such an embarrassment, especially to those without cars.

Before a Speaker leaves, quietly check whether there were any unexpected but unavoidable extra expenses; complete the already countersigned cheque; put it into an addressed envelope, tuck in the flap for safety and hand it over to her unostentatiously but with renewed thanks. As soon as possible she should examine it and if there had been any misunderstanding, get it put right while still on the premises.

COMMITTEE AS SUCH

The Committe is responsible for the day-to-day running of the group and the achieving of its specific aims. The officers could manage on their own at least for a time but members like to be in on the action so some non-officers are always elected to represent 'public opinion'.

Though a Committee may discuss anything, its powers to act may be limited by the Rules. Any action beyond these limits would be deemed *ultra vires* (pronounced *UL-tra VI-reez* and meaning 'outside their powers' from the phrase 'beyond the strength of'). However, having wide powers to act, it can be called an Executive Committee, which is sometimes shortened to The Executive, but as this title might mean just one individual, abbreviation is usually to The Committee.

How many members make up a committee and how long do they serve? The facetious remark that the most efficient committee consists of three people, two of whom live abroad, contains much practical wisdom but crises apart, would not long be tolerated by an active group. To be continually effective, a Committee needs to draw on a wide and frequently-changing range of experience, age, location, occupation or whatever categories are relevant while keeping to manageable numbers. Sometimes the Committee has to be large. A group with several components such as a Historical, Geographical, Geological and Archeological Society must give all parts equal voice lest there be mutterings of secession. Committees consisting largely of representatives of many sub-committees might be unwieldy if there were also many elected members as such. The only possible guide to the optimum size for any particular Committee is that it should efficiently reflect the needs of that particular group.

If it has stopped doing that, the Rules should be changed.

All main and most auxiliary officers are members of the Committee but only rarely are all Committee members officers and, their Committee functions being different, elected Committee members have different 'conditions of service' from officers. Often, officers with executive powers must submit themselves annually for re-election so that if they have not been functioning well they can be removed without delay. Sometimes Committee members also must submit themselves annually for re-election but often, to maintain continuity, they are elected for a continuous period of several years, retiring in rotation then either taking on the work of an officer or returning to 'the floor' for at least a year while they recharge with ideas. Later, any of them could quite properly serve another stint as a Committee member. Their period of continuous service varies but three years seems the most usual, being short enough to fit comfortably into many lifestyles but long enough to exhaust most people's store of contacts and ideas. Also, it fits into the size of many Committees for to get a smooth rotation the number of elected members must be related to the length of their service. A three-year term allows three or six elected members; a four-year stint would require four or eight.

Quorum

This is pronounced *KWOR-um*, from the word meaning 'of whom' or 'of which'. Ideally, all Committee members should attend all Committee meetings but in practice this does not happen and sometimes by ill-luck very few might attend or many leave early. Decisions taken by the rump of the Committee or by the few who had attended could be suspect, so almost all Rules specify the minimum number deemed to be reasonably representative. It is usually one-third to one-half the total voting Committee membership, must include at least one officer and requires that all members of the Committee had been notified of the meeting. This minimum acceptable number is called the quorum. Fantastic as it may seem to small, innocent, provincial study groups, the origin of this proviso is the need to guard against a 'coup' in which a small number of rebels might take over, perhaps by keeping a meeting going until most members had left. It is all part of the price of the wider freedoms.

Official business cannot be started until there is a quorum nor continue if it no longer exists. If a Chair sees how few people are present and how many apologies have been sent, she may immediately adjourn the meeting but is more likely to say sometime like 'As we seem not to have a quorum, I suggest we informally consider the matter of . . .'. No official business could be done and no Minutes be read or written up but notes of the discussion might be useful when the subject comes up officially. Eventually Chair says 'This meeting is adjourned until . . .' and arranges for all members of the Committee to be informed of the new date. If, then, there is still no quorum, valid decisions may be taken, but the wellbeing of that Committee would seem open to question.

Where should committees meet?

Committees mostly meet in private houses which, being available, welcoming, comfortable and rent-free are almost ideal, though the boon of available light refreshments has to be handled carefully. Fewer people will offer rooms if one-up-manship has taken hold. The variation of places from meeting to meeting helps spread the costs and also the nuisance of transport. As the furnishings will differ from home to home, different personal problems will be accommodated or emphasised, whether stiff knees or impaired hearing. When note-taking surfaces are adequate and there is no need to share documents, the varying seating arrangements can aid the conduct of the meeting by separating officers and so preventing the whispered confabs which sometimes disturb the smoothness of a discussion.

New members, wishing to do the correct thing and having heard they should stand to speak, soon find that if not many people are present, standing is not only unnecessary, it may be a time-wasting distraction, if armchairs are low and this causes a literal pain in the neck for the neighbour trying to look up into the face of the speaker standing at her elbow.

When should committees meet?

A Committee meets whenever it considers a meeting is necessary. Some like to get together before each business meeting to plan its details; some meet just after, to execute its instructions; some meet without regard to any other rhythm. Whatever the basis, dates are least likely to be forgotten if they have a pattern, for example, regularly on the first Tuesday of the month or the Monday before each business meeting, and are best fixed for the whole year while diaries are relatively blank. If a meeting is called at short notice, there is a risk that only two dates will be at all reasonable but that one of them is impossible for A and the other for B, so someone has to make a conspicuously invidious choice.

Whatever else it does, any Committee must meet just after the AGM so that the new people can take over officially, new officers reveal their hopes and new members learn the ways of that group. One of this meeting's jobs should be to check and correct the Minutes of the AGM. Official confirmation and signing must wait until the next AGM but by then few people will remember much of what happened so without this immediate check the accuracy of the Minutes would be difficult to sustain or rebut. Minutes of a meeting held some time previously can only be trusted if they were checked while memories were fresh.

The other essential meeting must be held a short while before the AGM to plan it and in particular to review the Reports and Accounts being presented by the Officers on behalf of that Committee. At it, the date for the post-AGM Committee should be provisionally fixed. It cannot be actually fixed for not until after the elections will the exact composition and therefore the exact availability of dates be known but mostly the majority of members do carry on over any particular year-end.

What is committee behaviour?

It is not a special drill invented for its own sake but is simply the exercise of good manners in special circumstances. For example, the 'rule' that only one person speaks at a time, uninterrupted, and that she addresses the Chair, is really just the most efficient way of getting business done quickly. However, there are points which deserve thought.

Starting promptly
Most Committee members prefer this to the ostensibly kind but actually lax delay until all are present, for that usually makes the start later and later.

Speaking formally
A veneer, however thin, of politeness and courtesy helps discussions to glide along smoothly and productively. This smoothness may be jarred by the thoughtless use of forenames. One new member may feel out in the cold if she is the only one addressed formally but another, realising that only such 'non-persons' as children and animals have to answer whatever name they are addressed by, will probably resent the familiarity! Anyway, there are practical problems. How can either of them pick out from an address list the 'Margaret' she is supposed to be writing to if the surname has not been in use and most members have an 'M' among their initials? However the others are addressed, there should be no doubt about officers who, if alluded to or addressed by their official title keep everyone aware of their respective responsibilities.

Maintaining Committee secrecy

Traditionally, Committee members have two apparently opposite aims. They are expected not to divulge committee secrets yet they are expected to inform members of the Committee's hopes and fears. The balance is not easy, as most people discover when they come off a committee and realise how little they can find out of what they ought to know. The problem of deciding what information should be broadcast is one of the most difficult to solve and all should be aware of it from the start, being guided by the knowledge that the secrecy 'rule' is needed as a guard against potential libel and is a way of enabling discussions to take place without fear of repercussions, as when someone who was expected to become an officer is planning to leave the district but does not want this widely known. She will expect other Committee members to protect her from pestering and yet not divulge the reason.

Quelling minor noises

In the quiet of a well-run meeting even the rustle of papers or the nervous clicking of a retractable pen can be disproportionately distracting. The maker of the noise may not notice it or even be able to hear it but it sets up a centre of unease unless dealt with promptly.

Eschewing passive spitting

Considering the established dislike of *active* spitting it is surprising that passive spitting is indulged in by so many people who, dealing with paper, lick their fingers to help separate the sheets. Not everyone likes being handed an Agenda only too tangibly moist with saliva, yet, without the saliva, what is the point of the gesture? Please avoid spitting!

Newly elected members

Newly elected members are a great asset, especially if not afraid to ask questions which at first may seem silly. The query 'why do we do that?' is one of the most useful and thought-provoking ever heard at a Committee meeting, for many activities outlast the need for them but old hands don't notice. A good Chair makes sure of a chat with any new members before they lose their valuable freshness of outlook. It is from them that she will get all sorts of ideas for future activities in a flourishing group or possibly of the group's incipient decay (but also might get her first hint of its renewed vigour). Nevertheless, a new Committee member does well to observe the oft-given advice to listen but not to speak during her first few meetings.

Co-opted members

Occasionally, a Committee lacks some expertise which might have been contributed by a particular member had she been available for election and been elected, so most Rules empower a Committee to co-opt, if they wish, a specified small number of extra members for specified reasons. A co-opted member is not elected by the AGM but chosen by the Committee at any of its meetings and serves only until the next AGM, unless again co-opted. The reason she never attends the first Committee of the year is simply that she could not have been constitutionally co-opted before it. She is almost always invited to all the other meetings if only because that is most convenient, but she might be asked to attend only when her expertise is likely to be required. She is not deemed an officer, does not count toward a quorum, does not vote on Committee, even on her own subject and though she may always speak on her own subject, on others may do so only with permission though, as she is an honoured member, normally it is given.

Casual vacancies

These are those which occur unexpectedly between elections. Unless Rules give some other guidance, the place would be filled by the Committee at one of their next meetings but would become vacant again at the next AGM. If that member is then elected routinely, her term of office would usually start from the AGM.

Sub-Committees

Sub-Committees are sometimes called Working Parties. Most executive Committees save their members' time by seeing that special jobs such as collecting data or organising particular activities are done by sub-Committees. The main Committee will have defined the sub-Committee's exact aims and powers, that is, its Terms of Reference, its Brief (as in Law circles) or its remit (in this context pronounced *RE-mit* not *re-MIT*). These include the expected time and frequency of reporting back to the main Committee (possibly every Committee meeting, certainly when the job is done or the AGM pending); the name of its Convenor who will Chair all its meetings and be responsible for its work to the main Committee; possibly the names of at least some of its members of whom most will come from the floor, though the Convenor might be left free to choose her own helpers; and whether it may itself co-opt and if so how many and whether from outside the group. Officers are *ex officio* members of all sub-Committees and sometimes attend meetings though mainly as observers, noting the progress of project or people (sub-committee work being an excellent sieve for possible future officers).

Every sub-Committee is likely to need at least a little of the group's money and some notepaper.

Standing Committee

A Standing Committee is a semi-permanent set of members, usually specialists, concerned with a single aspect of the group's main work, for example, a Charity money-raising sub-Committee or a Civic Society's Architects' and Planners' Working Party. Most groups also have a Standing Committee which takes responsibility for all catering. A Standing Committee is re-appointed at each AGM though not necessarily with the same members or even the same Convenor, though only rarely is the term of service limited beforehand.

Ad hoc Committee

Ad hoc, pronounced *ADD-HOCK*, is from the phrase meaning when complete 'to this purpose only' and means a Committee that is quite temporary, appointed to do one particular job and then automatically dissolved, though the same set of people may be appointed again to do some other particular job or jobs. This may be something big, such as running a really large dinner dance, but is particularly suited to sorting out just one small idea.

TAKING OFFICIAL DECISIONS

Conferences

Many Organisations hold Conferences to discover their members' views on matters of topical concern. Most such meetings are open to all members (space permitting) but usually only recognised Representatives, chosen according to the prevailing Rules, may speak or vote. Customarily every branch is allowed at least one Representative, its other members being classed as Observers, non-speaking and non-voting. All feel most involved when free to sit where they wish, Observers collecting around their Representative for brief consultations and Speakers trying to make sure everyone can hear them. However, vote-counting is undoubtedly easier when all Representatives sit in one group, separated from Observers.

Months before a Conference, HQ tells branches which subjects are to be debated so that members can study them. In the subsequent discussion everyone who wishes can bring at least a trace of influence to bear on the eventual debate and vote, her views being explained by her Representative to the others at the Conference. Later, everyone can learn more about the subject under the spotlight from the returned Representative's description of the course of the debate.

Usually, when a Representative is registered at HQ for the Conference, she is sent a coloured card to hold up when voting. If, after all, she cannot attend, HQ can allow another (named) member of that branch to replace her, hold the branch's card and express its views, as well as contributing her own experience. Though a replacement, she can add significantly to the richness of the debate, but unfortunately that significance is often played down.

Instead of being given the title of *Alternative* Voter she is sometimes called a *Proxy*, though that term belongs rather to organisations in which every member has a vote and to the business world where views can more easily be set out in print and circularised and where swings of opinion are not to be expected during meetings. Then, when votes rather than views are solicited, a member who cannot attend may empower a member who will be there to exercise both votes (but take no other action on behalf of the absentee), that is, she acts as proxy.

Two other words used in Conference discussions are often also confused. These are 'Delegate' and 'Representative'. A *Representative* listens to the views and opinions of her branch but is expected to use her own brains and to weigh up the facts and views revealed during the debate, together with those of her branch, before she decides how to vote. A *Delegate* is a kind of walking postal voter, mandated by her branch and bound by them not to change, no matter how cogent the opposing arguments, thus undermining one of the purposes of holding a Conference.

However, unless an organisation's Articles of Association describe Conferences as a legal entity, final responsibility for Resolutions cannot lie with it, however overwhelmingly accepted. Each Resolution must still be considered by whatever body (usually the AGM) is officially defined as being responsible in law for the actions and pronouncements of that organisation. Only if that body ratifies a Resolution does it become official policy.

Ratification of Conference Resolutions, decisions concerning the organisation's own functioning or a Proposition put forward by any group are almost always taken by the AGM, that is by at least a quorum of members, formally assembled and already informed of the business to be conducted, who, therefore, are seen to be jointly responsible for all decisions in law and in the eyes of the world. Virtually all sets of Rules ensure this by stipulating that a general Meeting must be held annually and listing some of the conditions governing that meeting and at least some of the matters which must be considered at it, and which I will describe later.

Additional decision-taking meetings

Extraordinary General Meeting
Occasionally an important decision is required between AGMs. Then a kind of extension of the AGM principle can be arranged, keeping to its rules of voting etc, but discussing just the one item. The Minutes of such meetings become part of the AGM stream, read together with those of the previous AGM at the next AGM. If real need ever arises, go ahead and call such an Extraordinary General Meeting, whether or not the possibility is mentioned in your Rules.

Special General Meeting
Most Rules do include a proviso (though it is rarely invoked) that a Special General Meeting must be called if a specified number of members send in a written request for a discussion of a specified matter, and it must be held within a specified period after the arrival of the request. The notice stating the place, date and time of the meeting must also state the reason it has been called, preferably in the exact words of the original request. There is nothing more determinedly democratic than a fully organised group and this proviso is a way of giving members a measure of control over their officers' activities, and any who are unsure of the acceptability of their recent actions should consider taking their books to the meeting ready to resign, for very often a discussion called in this way ends up by lancing a boil, so to speak.

Sometimes an annual cycle of activity needs to mesh with a differently geared annual cycle, as when organisations which lobby Governments have to time their policy-making Conference so that the decisions fit in with the Parliamentary season, though their own AGM would be best held at some quite different part of the year. Formal responsibility for Conference decisions must be taken under AGM Rules and this can be done by holding a Special General Meeting as soon as the Conference itself finishes. The AGM itself can then be held at the ideal time.

Annual General Meeting

This is often the only meeting actually mentioned in the Rules and it has all the makings of a really special occasion, particularly when there is a stipulation that only members may attend it. The reason for this proviso is that the presence of non-members almost automatically stifles comment yet criticism which is continually suppressed tends to rumble on under the surface, festering and often leading to either explosions or apathy. Members will more willingly take an active part in the discussions when on their own. Criticism can be given and taken without repercussions and troubles be aired yet kept 'in the family'; praise offered when (though only when) it is merited can be publicised later. Such unfettered discussion is essential for any group which hopes to keep its routines out of ruts and its members active, rather than just sources of subscriptions.

AGMs necessarily differ in detail from one year to another and from one group or organisation to another, but the general pattern is always much the same. For Rules always stipulate much the same items and common sense requires them to be considered in much the same sequence. Most of the matters dealt with have to be prepared simultaneously and often there is overlap even during the meeting itself so, to prevent confusion, I will describe the various subjects separately, then summarise the whole meeting in Agenda order.

Reports
Between them, officers' reports to an AGM should

summarise every aspect of what they and the Committee have done on the members' behalf during that year. Mostly the picture is made more vivid and complete by being given from several points of view in several voices without much actual repetition, for all should have been written in collaboration. Mostly there are three reports, one given by each main officer, but deputies who take on real responsibility can speak with an authority which often justifies the slight extra fuss and movement of additional speakers. By contrast, when most of the work is done by officials, as in many of the larger organisations, it is the custom for just one person to deal with all aspects in one speech.

Written reports can be immediately filed as part of the official records but if given extempore, they must be summarised in the Minutes, care being taken to get the nub of each. A future student will learn little from reading, for example, 'The Hon Secretary gave a most interesting account of this busy year'.

With her own report coming later in the Agenda, the *Chair's* opening welcome should have been warm but brief. Her actual report should be a non-statistical, non-financial review of the year as she saw it. She mentions her pleasure in the various activities (or, very occasionally, has to voice some displeasure), her enjoyment of having represented the group at one event, her welcome of an eminent visitor to another. She outlines the year, others fill in the details.

Each group must decide the sequence of the other reports which best suits them, always remembering that this is an AGM. Most other meetings make plans for the future, and members need to know how much money they have before considering how to spend it. The AGM is different. It looks backward at, among other things, money which has been spent. Members are more interested in what has been done with the money than in how much was spent, so usually the Secretary speaks after Chair, dealing with the statistics of membership, with meeting places and meetings and whatever has mainly occupied the time of that group. If there happens to have been any important correspondence, she usually brings it into her Report.

Finally, the Treasurer comments on her Statement of Accounts. If members have copies of this she probably adds little beyond offering to explain puzzling items, an offer which should be taken up if only for the benefit of those members who do not themselves understand enough to put a question. Should this Report include out-standingly good or especially depressing news, this is her opportunity to emphasise and explain it and to use her statistics to support whatever financial recommendations she makes.

Two other items stipulated by most Rules for mention at the AGM are linked with the Treasurer. The subscription for the year has to be fixed and this is often the culmination of her report. Then, every item of direct financial importance having been dealt with, the Auditor whose integrity has underpinned it all must be thanked and either re-appointed or her successor discussed.

Elections

Elections are organised by the Returning Officer, often the Hon Secretary wearing a different hat. You must make provision for all four stages of the election, always keeping to your Rules. You must arrange for vacancies to be correctly identified; enable people willing to serve in them to be found and nominated; give members the opportunity to choose among these candidates; and see that their choice is announced.

Which vacancies exist? Consult your Rules. In groups which permit unlimited periods of service, vacancies are rare and unpredictable. In many groups, annual re-election is required up to stated maximum periods. Some groups provide that a few members of the Committee shall be elected to serve for several years without re-election, the various people retiring in rotation. In addition, members' circumstances sometimes cause premature retirement so, as the AGM approaches, ask each member of Committee who is not constitutionally barred whether she is willing to continue.

You can easily identify all but the unscheduled retirements if you keep a list of all Committee places and their constitutional requirements and, after each AGM, add the name of each incumbent. Use this register to compile an information sheet ready to send to your voting members with their nomination forms (for only voters may nominate). My example of Information Sheet and Nomination Form would fit many groups but might be totally out of accord with your Rules and practice. You might, for example, still require a seconder for each nomination. On the nomination form always state all vacancies and leave one space beside each for the nominator to write, legibly, the name of her nominee; another space for that nominee to sign her agreement to serve if elected; leave space somewhere for the nominator to state her own name; and give the address to which the form should be returned and the final date for this.

Who may vote? Consult your Rules. Large organistions sometimes have special patterns of voting. In small groups usually only paid up members of categories who have voting rights and are present may vote.

Candidates may vote and should do so in their own favour. (If they did not consider themselves capable of doing the job they should not have accepted nomination.) Having accepted nomination, not to vote for themselves would impugne the proposer's judgement (and no candidate should withdraw without the agreement of her nominator).

Tellers' voting rights are not affected by their responsibilities as Tellers. Chair's voting rights are as stated in the Rules. Some groups consider she should retain her voting rights as a member, some that while she is in the Chair she should be unbiased. Either way, whoever is in the Chair is

HERE AND THERE SOCIETY
NOMINATION SHEET

Present Committee

Chair:	Miss J. Austen	Has served one year in this office, is eligible for re-election for 2 more years and is willing to be re-nominated.
Past Chair:	Mrs A. Norris	
Deputy Chair:	Dr M.Crawford	Has served three years in this office and is not eligible for re-election to it.
Acting Hon Secretary:	Mrs Clay	Is eligible for election to any office and is willing to serve in any.
Hon Treasurer:	Lady Russell	Has served one year in this office. Does not wish to be re-nominated as she is moving from the district.
Deputy Hon Treasurer:	Miss M. Grant	Has served one year in this office and is eligible for re-election for 2 more years or for service in other offices, and is willing to be nominated.

Miss S. Croft
Mrs J. Musgrove } were elected one year ago to serve for three years so are due to serve two or more years without re-election.

Miss Bingley
Miss F. Price } were elected two years ago to serve for three years. Miss Price is unable to complete her term so a vacancy exists.

Mrs P. Bertram
Mrs M. Lucas } were elected three years ago to serve for three years so are not eligible for re-election as Committee members.

PLEASE BRING THIS SHEET TO THE AGM

NOMINATION FORM

Nominations are needed for all officers (except Past Chair), 2 Committee members to serve for three years and one to serve for one year. Nominator and each nominee must be paid up voting members. The two nominees as elected Committee members who gain the highest numbers of votes will be asked to serve for three years, the one with the next highest number, asked to serve for one year only.

OFFICE	NAME OF NOMINEE	NOMINEE'S SIGNATURE
		of agreement to serve if elected

Chair . . . .

Deputy Chair . . . .

Hon Secretary . . . .

Hon Treasurer . . . .

Committee members . . . .

. . . .

. . . .

Signature of nominator . . . .

Please send completed form to Returning Officer at The High School by Dec 31st.

the only one who can break a tie in voting so she always has a casting vote though, in a secret ballot, none but the Tellers should know whether it is ever exercised, and Tellers don't tell.

Dealing with nomination forms Don't worry if not many are returned. What matters is not a plethora of forms but a sufficiency of names. As each paper arrives check its validity, making sure that all names are of voting members and that all required signatures are included. If the nominator has not signed, the whole form is invalid; if an individual nominee has not signed her agreement to serve, that nomination cannot be accepted but others on that form may still be valid. Keep invalid forms aside until after the AGM in case of challenge.

Make your own 'master form', a spare combined Information sheet and Nomination form generally being the most convenient. Enter on the relevant line each fresh valid nomination. When there is one name for each vacancy you know there will be a full working Committee next year. When there is a second name on at least one line, start to prepare for an election. If there are to be elections for several vacancies, prepare to discuss their timing with Chair.

Until the stipulated date, all valid nominations must be accepted; after it, only if there is a vacancy may any fresh names be considered and only until each vacancy is filled. Even as late as the AGM itself, the first valid nomination must be accepted and no other so if, by the stipulated date, the list is not absolutely full, change your routine. Still setting aside invalid forms in their own batch, start keeping any others strictly in the order of their arrival. Look only for nominations for the vacant place(s), accepting the first nomination (only) for each. If the space continues empty, drop a hint to the Committee. They will almost certainly be willing to put forward a name before the AGM. At worst, the space can be treated as a casual vacancy after the AGM.

At the last practicable moment, reprograph the list of

nominations if that is your custom or make fair copies of it for your Chair, the Tellers and yourself. If necessary, discuss with Chair how to adjust the Agenda to fit the elections and who might be suitable as Tellers, arrangements which will depend upon just which vacancies need filling and who has been nominated. Take the nomination forms to the AGM in case of challenge, still in their valid and invalid bundles in date order if relevant. After the meeting, burn them.

When no election is needed If in any year there is only one nomination for each vacancy, no special arrangements need be made. When the item 'Tellers' is reached, Chair will announce something like 'This year no Tellers seem to be needed' and pass on to the next item. At the item 'Elections' she says, quite simply and without false modesty 'There being only one nomination for each vacancy, the people who have been returned unopposed to serve on the Committee for the next year are . . .' and reads out the list starting with her own name. She then says 'May I have a show of hands that this Committee is acceptable to you'. This converts a negative kind of arrangement into a positive set of nominations.

Note the terminology. A person is either elected or returned unopposed. No-one can be elected unopposed.

Whenever an election is needed Whenever an election is needed discuss the choice of Tellers with Chair and sound out at least two possible choices, asking them to wear silent heels in case they do have to move about during discussions. Tellers are so called because they keep tally of votes. Originally Scrutineers planned and supervised, Tellers collected and counted, but Tellers seem to have taken over.

Election results matter, so in principle, the group's whole future depends upon the integrity of the Tellers so they must be acceptable to the group as a whole. Supervision of their work by the group being quite impossible, they normally act in pairs, each the guarantor of the other. A Teller should be honest, numerate, willing to work with the partner and to follow the Chair's instructions, not a nominee nor a close connection of any nominee and preferably not a continuing member of Committee. Paragons are rare but usually it is possible to find enough reasonably suitable people, possibly those about to retire from the Committee or even non-voting members. Check that they would be willing to act but remember that it should be the members themselves who put forward names when Chair asks for them.

If any suitable nominations are made, Chair should welcome them, but most members know that almost certainly provisional arrangements have been made and will gladly let the Chair suggest names, As she does so, articulating them clearly, she should ask all proposed Tellers in turn to stand. They should be upstanding at least long enough to be recognised by all. When accepted by a show of hands (with no dissenters) they should be prepared to count votes when asked and possibly do other jobs as well. While waiting they should count the voting members present for later comparison with the number of voting papers collected.

Unless each member has a complete list of nominations, try to arrange for a blackboard to be visible to all, with the nominees listed in alphabetical order of surname. Except where she can be confident that everyone knows all the candidates by appearance and surname, a tactful Chair will have made sure that each nominee does some small job among the members in the earlier part of the meeting, addressing her by the name appearing on the list so that people can more readily identify the nominees, for example 'Miss Elliott, would you mind distributing these papers for me, please'. All candidates for election must be given equivalent opportunities.

When the Elections item is reached, Chair asks each candidate in turn to stand. (She should do so for long enough to satisfy any who need to adjust their glasses to both the name on the board and to the person.) When all have been identified, Chair will instruct members to write the names of their chosen nominee(s) on the papers being given out.

By then the Tellers will be distributing blank pieces of paper to everyone, including the platform. Each Teller, if she is also a voter, fills in her own paper, folds it and drops it into the bowl she now holds, then moves about the hall and along the platform holding out her bowl to collect the folded papers. When no more seem to be coming, Chair will rise, ask for any other papers to be given in quickly and before chatter can start again, move on to the next item on the Agenda.

Tellers go to a scheduled place and count the papers as they unfold them, discarding as invalid any which are illegible or have too many names. If, as is just possible, there are more valid papers than voters present, they should ask for a re-vote. If there are fewer papers than expected, they should check that none has fallen to the floor but need not worry further. Valid voting is rarely compulsory.

More than one nomination for one vacancy Chair will ask members to write one name only on their voting paper. Tellers should sort the papers into piles, a different name in each and count the papers in each pile. The successful candidate is the one with most votes. This name (not the number of votes unless specifically instructed) should be written clearly on thick paper which cannot be read from the wrong side and folded once. While one Teller returns to her seat the other quietly puts the folded paper in front of the Chair, then also sits. At the next logical break, Chair will look at it and announce 'Our new Committee member is . . . We welcome her'.

Just occasionally the Tellers (only), will be aware that an extra decision has been made. If there is a tie between candidates' votes, the tied names will be written in alphabetical order of surname and, to avoid misunderstanding, bracketed, with the word TIE added eg

Miss Thorpe		
Miss Tilney	}	Tie

Chair, knowing it is her duty to give a casting vote when necessary, will have made up her mind beforehand and will give her choice without hesitation, this method of setting out the results making sure that none but the Tellers know of the tie and, 'Tellers don't tell'.

If the incumbent Chair is a candidate In this case it is customary for her to stand down for the time being. Not that she could bring much influence to bear but justice should, wherever possible, be seen to be done. When the 'Elections' item is reached on the Agenda, she asks permission of the meeting to vacate the Chair, for if she starts to move about for no apparent reason, members who are not awake to the situation might start to worry about possible illness. She also suggests another officer to take her place, but as it is not the prerogative of the Chair to decide who else might run the meeting she must get the permission of members to make this change. Agreement given, they physically change places. They also change voting rights and duties. The voting rights of the Chair now accrue to the Acting Chair, including her responsibility for giving a casting vote. Chair herself, whatever her previous constitutional position, is now expected to exercise one vote.

The Acting Chair makes sure there is no favouritism by announcing each candidate, asking them to stand, indicating the names (alphabetically by surname) on the board and inviting members to write down the one they want, then, with votes collected, she moves on to the next item on the Agenda, (having, if necessary been briefed beforehand). Only when she has glanced at the paper brought by the Teller and announced the result of that stage of the election will she resume her original place and voting rights. The original Chair also resumes her place and rights and continues the meeting.

When there are two or more similar vacancies and several candidates For members, the routine is much the same as for a vacancy between two candidates except that Chair asks them to write as many names as there are vacancies. For Tellers, the routine is different. Each draws up a checklist with as many columns as there are candidates and heads each column with a candidate's name. Having counted the papers and removed any which are invalid, one Teller reads out from each paper each name in turn, putting a light stroke through that name while doing so. The other puts a mark in that candidate's column. The pile of papers finished, they change jobs, the marker reading, the reader marking her own checklist. All columns are added up and totals compared. The two checklists should tally. As before, if there is a clear answer, sufficient names having more votes than others, those names are written in alphabetical order, the paper folded and taken to the Chair. If there is a tie at the borderline it must always be shown clearly. The names of those who are safely elected are written as a group in order of surnames and bracketed then, separately, the names of those who have tied, eg

Miss Bennet,
Miss Eliott, } elected and one of   Miss Crawford } Tied
Mrs Price,   Mrs Norris

Some Chairs prefer to ask members to vote again between those who tied. This saves Chair from taking immediate responsibility but leaves everyone aware that there was a tie somewhere and may still not settle the problem.

When a candidate is named for more than one vacancy Organisations and very large groups often require specialists in office but in smaller groups any candidate could probably be equally successful in almost any of the offices. Different people may approach a good candidate, asking her to act in various offices or simply on the Committee. The voting may be mainly influenced by the strength or weaknesses of opposing candidates so an election for all places simultaneously would probably split votes and produce results satisfactory to no-one.

Groups which are fortunate enough to have a choice of potential officers do well to take their elections in stages, in descending order of importance of officers in that group. Chair first, followed by the Treasurer in money-raising groups, but the Secretary in others. With the names of all candidates for all the vacancies listed on the blackboard or member's papers so all can sum up the situation for themselves, the first stage is carried out as soon after the reports as possible as a straightforward election, possibly for Chair. That decided, the name of the successful candidate is rubbed off the board or crossed off members' lists wherever it had appeared. If this leaves two or more names for the next office, another stage of the election is held, choosing between these; another name is erased everywhere and so down the list until all places are filled. The other business of the meeting is continued between the stages unless a long interval can be declared, perhaps for tea.

Block voting Block voting is probably never to be advocated though sometimes it is suggested when several people have worked together successfully as a Committee for quite a time despite, or even in accord with, the Rules. If eventually one of them moves from the district and more than one nomination is received for the vacant place, there must be an election.

There may be a move to re-elect the remaining Committee en bloc in tribute to their past excellence and to complete the numbers by electing one from among the nominees. Always resist this. Justice will not be done and it will be seen not to be done unless all have equal chance of being elected. The election might, in fact, be an opportunity to clear away some dead wood.

Finally, every vacancy having been filled, the Minutes Secretary will have listed the new officers and Committee members and these will be preparing to become active members of Committee but not before the end of the meeting, when they assume responsibility. The Press Secretary will be preparing to inform local newspapers and HQ. Your job as Returning Officer will be complete as soon as you have burnt the various nomination forms and voting papers.

Motions and Resolutions

These are the main business of policy-making Conferences and may play an important part in the AGM of any group. Effective Motions arise from burning convictions but the convictions and the supporting research are outside the scope of a book on Committees, as are the techniques of composing or delivering the necessary speeches. However, the wording of Motions, methods of voting in general and of declaring results do come within our ambit.

Wording A Motion stands or falls not by its intention but by its wording so this must be quite precise. Wise drafters try out proposed wordings on one person after another until everyone who reads or hears it freshly gets the impression intended. This way of experimenting has culminated in a kind of universally understood formula. Let's take as an illustration an imaginary example from the past.

VOTES FOR WOMEN

. . . That the Here-and-There Society in Conference assembled, noting the high level of disturbance arising from the continued disenfranchisement of women, urges HM Secretary of State for Home Affairs to introduce legislation during the current session of parliament to provide for universal adult franchise.

The descriptive Short Title 'Votes for Women' enables it to be picked out easily from a list. The format, beginning with the word '. . . That . . .' is the logical continuation from the proposer's implied traditional opening phrase 'I beg to move . . .', a phrase which has itself produced the generic title of 'Motions'.

Motions become Resolutions when, but only when, they have been accepted (much as Bills become Acts when they have passed all parliamentary stages). The Motion quoted is an example to be followed in having a single objective; one which is not just pie in the sky but is capable of implementation. It is precisely and unambiguously stated in impeccable English with no abbreviations such as eg or etc, or words which no longer have an exact meaning (should, may, might). It has no jargon or confusion of negatives. It states the change desired and the reason for the request; includes in its wording both the title of the organisation putting it forward and the status of the meeting which debated it; it is addressed to the office which could be responsible for implementing it. Altogether, it is complete; misunderstanding is surely impossible.

Voting Voting can be secret, fast or accurate but not all at once, even when Chair has repeated the proposition clearly and accurately. There are several possible methods.

1) A paper ballot is secret, so it is used for elections but not often otherwise, for it does take time.

2) Acclaim, when most members spontaneously rise, shouting their approval, gives an immediate answer but it is neither secret nor accurate. Anyway, such excitement is rare outside political meetings.

3) A voice vote is rapid and easy but may not be decisive. It mostly happens when the question 'shall we?' received a murmured 'yes' or 'no' but if both can be heard fairly equally, a more accurate count ought to be taken.

4) 'Show of hands' is the slowest, the most wearying but

the most accurate method, especially when coloured voting cards have been issued so that empty hands can be ignored.

There are three stages in any vote. These are a) those in favour of the Motion, b) those against and c) those abstaining. The count of abstentions is a check on the arithmetic for the three sets of votes ought together to equal, but should certainly never exceed the number of voters present. Sometimes it also gives an indication of the strength or lack of conviction behind the reaction to a proposition. Few would put much faith in a Resolution passed because its proposer and seconder voted for it and no-one voted against it but everyone else abstained.

As always, Chair has a casting vote and if there is a tie, must show she has used it. Always it should be in favour of the status quo (pronounced *STAT-us KWO* from the phrase meaning 'previous position') if only because a change opposed by half the members is unlikely to succeed.

Results However defined and by whatever method or ratio, any decision arrived at democratically is binding on all, including those who voted against it, abstained or even were not present. The results themselves, elections apart, are often announced by description whatever the method of voting.

1) Unanimous means that everyone present and qualified to vote has done so and in the same direction; none voted in the contrary direction and none abstained.

2) An overwhelming majority shows that a few did abstain or vote in the contrary way but so few that counting seemed unnecessary.

3) Carried 'nem con' (a shortened form of 'nemine contradictione' meaning, literally, no-one contradicting) looks like high praise and usually is, but may mean that many were too unsure of the effect or the meaning of the

proposition to vote in its favour but had not the confidence to vote against it.

4) A majority is self-explanatory, but

5) A bare majority means that a difference of just one vote can determine the result.

6) A statement of numbers of votes cast. This method is used when Rules require that more than a bare majority must be cast in favour, a frequent proviso for changes of constitution, or, in Conference, for policy decisions. Then, a majority is required of at least two-thirds of those present, entitled to vote and voting. It is not easy to judge from a show of hands whether such a vote will or will not be passed. Counting is essential.

Conduct of the debate

As might be expected, there is usually a time limit set for all Speakers in a debate, the first, the Proposer of the Motion, being expected to repeat the proposition verbatim before the clock is started. She sticks to her subject but does not cover it entirely having, by arrangement, left some aspects to her Seconder who does not repeat the proposition. It is then thrown open to general debate, speeches for and against being called alternately, if possible, until the discussion is stopped for lack of speakers with fresh points of view or because time has run out. The Proposer (only) is allowed a few minutes to exercise her 'right of reply', that is to explain or define matters which have arisen during the debate. She may not introduce new matter. Finally, the vote is taken.

Major amendments Even when the principle and most of the wording of a Motion are approved, there may be disagreement over some phrase or number, so a routine has been evolved by which the wording may be amended (ie changed slightly) to make the proposition more acceptable rather than having to abandon the whole thing. The example I have chosen is more extreme and intricate than is ever likely to occur in practice but it does bring in most aspects of amendments.

Original Motion This is the version printed in the Agenda. It might read 'That the Here-And-There Society donate £60 to the Mayor's Fund'. Wording and principle seem, by early speeches, to be acceptable. However, the Mayor administers several Funds and someone, remembering this, prepares to suggest an amendment.

Proposal of amendment She catches the eye of Chair (or passes up a signed card) saying 'I would like to move, as an amendment, that the word 'Distress' be inserted before the word 'Fund''. Chair makes sure this proposal has a Seconder then asks the Proposer and Seconder of the original Motion if they accept the change. They may be glad to for proposers should not themselves suggest amendments though unofficially changes such as this one do get made. If they do not object, Chair turns to the members and says 'An Amendment has been proposed that the word 'Distress' be inserted before the word 'Fund' and has been accepted by the Movers of the Motion. Will you accept this amendment without debate?'

Vote on accepting the amendment undebated There may be a sufficient murmur of agreement for the Chair to continue confidently with the changed wording but acceptance cannot be taken for granted. Some members may see good reason for the original choice of words.

Temporarily the original Motion is set aside and so is any consideration of its substance. Without any further speeches a vote is taken on the simple Yes/No choice. 'Hands up those who want to debate the amendment', 'Hands up those who accept the amendment without debating it'. That is all this vote is about. It is nothing to do with Funds or Mayors. If the doubters win there must be a debate on the inclusion of the word 'Distress'.

Debate and vote on the amendment (Note this is on the amendment that the word 'Distress' be included.) The proposer of the amendment explains why she moved it; others explain why they wish the Mayor to have discretion and a vote is taken. At this stage members are deciding whether, *if* money is sent it shall be to an unspecified Fund or specifically to the Distress Fund so, if passed, the substantive Motion, as it is called, becomes 'That . . . £60 to be given to the Mayor's Distress Fund' and each member inserts the word 'Distress' in her own copy. If negatived, the word 'Distress' is not heard of again.

Non-adopted second amendment If, during the debate on the inclusion of the word 'Distress', someone had said 'I would like to propose as an amendment that only £30, and not £60 be given', the Chair would reply 'I cannot accept two amendments at the same time, later I will consider accepting yours', that is, the suggested amendment seemed intrinsically valid but must be postponed until the first is resolved.

Acceptance of second amendment The first amendment resolved, that £30 replaces £60 in the original Motion is again proposed, and can be accepted by Chair.

Amendment to this amendment Free now to think about money, another member might propose that the figure in the Motion be £100. This seems to be a second amendment but as it is still the same figure (or word) under discussion it is not a second, a separate, amendment but an amendment to an amendment and entirely acceptable. There are now several ideas floating round and at first sight it seems an impossible task to debate and choose between them by vote but as usual, the traditional routine reduces the voting to a series of yes/no decisions each concerning one point only. This is managed by (perhaps surprisingly) taking the amendments in the reverse order of their proposal, that is, working backward.

Vote on the amendment to the second amendment There being no more amendments to that amendment, the meeting debates and votes on the most recent of the ideas put before it, that the figure be £100 (that is, that *if* a gift is made it should be for £100. Nothing else is under consideration, not even whether the gift will eventually be made. Votes concerned with amendments should never assume that the original Motion, amended or not, will in the end be accepted). Those who do want £100 to be given will vote for it. Everyone else will vote against — those who wish for £30, those who wish for £60 and also those who are against giving anything at all. If more votes are in favour of £100 it becomes the substantive sum and all other figures can be crossed out. There would be no point in voting on £30 or £60 for, in effect, they have already been outvoted. If the £100 (that is the amendment to the amendment) is negatived, it is the £100 which is crossed out and is not heard of again.

Debate and vote on the original second amendment that £30 be the sum mentioned. Working backward, the next idea which must be considered is the original second amendment, that is that *if* a gift is made, shall it or shall it not be £30. After discussion as to its merits, everyone votes afresh. If those in favour of £30 are in the majority the amendment has been carried and the substantive Motion becomes 'That this group donate £30 to the Mayor's Distress Fund'. If this vote is not carried the substantive Motion is as at first, the sum being £60.

Debate and vote on substantive Motion One question remains, that of whether a gift is to be made at all? People have talked all round it but the central question has not yet come up for discussion. Had someone at any stage proposed as an amendment 'That no gift be made' that proposal would not have been accepted. A direct opposite is never acceptable as an amendment for the same result is reached much less confusingly by simply voting against the Motion. So now, all alternatives having been outvoted, at last the substantive Motion can be discussed and voted on, that is, Do you, or do you not want a gift to be made? If made it will certainly be for the amount already determined and be sent to the Fund already determined.

Those in favour . . . , those against . . . , those abstaining, and at last the whole question is resolved.

In practice even a large meeting is unlikely to have taken as long as reading it suggests and in small meetings or Committees judgement would certainly have been based on tone of voice or the occasional interjection, usually enough to show, with no need for voting, which details were and which were not acceptable, but the course of the discussion would have been much the same.

Speeding the debate

Even when the length of speeches is firmly controlled, members do sometimes get impatient, especially if the arguments are confused, so routines have developed for cutting through muddles and for speeding things up, sometimes even forcing the hand of an overly-patient Chair.

Most people are familiar with the more straightforward routines, such as invoking points of order, but a glance into a book on the art of debating may well be puzzling because of esoteric routines sometimes described and not least because of their unlikely titles. Don't worry about them. The kind of ruthless device which might permanently banish a Motion is basically political, a 'spoiling tactic' which has no place in the kind of meeting this book caters for. However, to give an idea of what is involved I have described them. Read through the details then forget all about any but the simplest.

Point of Order A 'Point of Order' deals with an emergency. Any worried member may at any time stand and say 'Mme Chair, on a point of order . . .' then, perhaps, 'Did the Secretary say she would, or she would not?' Or, on another occasion, perhaps, 'May we have lights'. A well-timed, well-phrased interjection is only a momentary interruption. It may disrupt a train of thought, but is likely to prevent much confusion later. Neither seconder nor vote is required and Chair need not accept the interruption but must give her ruling immediately one way or another, for nothing else can happen until she has done so.

Proposal by Chair Occasionally when a debate has consisted largely of repetition, with very slight variation, a normally neutral Chair might interrupt it by summarising it in a proposition of her own and putting this immediately to the vote. A proposal from the Chair does not need a seconder, the assumption being that she only does this when she is confident of overwhelming support, so that most of the queue of speakers would willingly have seconded her proposal.

Referring back If discussion of a worthy subject has got bogged down it may be because the wording is bad. If so, someone should propose that the Motion (or Amendment) be referred back for re-drafting. This proposal needs a seconder and a vote. If defeated, the discussion continues as if uninterrupted. If carried, the Motion must be immediately withdrawn, as is right and proper. No Motion should be allowed to take up members' time unless the wording is above reproach. There is no implied proviso that the re-worded version will ever be accepted. It will be so only on its own merits.

'That the question be now put' This speeds things up when no new views are being put forward and people seem to have made up their minds how to vote. If Chair seems too patient, a less tolerant member (never the Proposer or Seconder of the original Motion) stands up and says 'Mme Chair, I propose that the question be now put'. If Chair accepts this proposition and it is seconded, the interjection (not yet the original question) must immediately be put to the vote. If defeated the debate goes on from where it was interrupted. If carried, the only speech permitted before that vote is the original proposer's Right of Reply.

Next business If someone from the floor, losing all patience, stands and interrupts speeches with the words 'Mme Chair, I propose the next business' and this is accepted by Chair and seconded it must immediately be put to the vote, without discussion. If defeated, debate goes from where it was interrupted; if accepted, the item under discussion is simply abandoned and everything moves on one step, that is, from amendment to main Motion or from one Motion to another. Being so wasteful and confusing in every way, it is rightly rarely invoked.

'Previous question' This is very drastic. It is occasionally used as the only way of dealing with a frivolous Motion which the mover refuses to withdraw but may be the only way of getting out of a tricky situation where the alternative might be utter embarrassment or a mass resignation of most members. To say 'Mme Chair, I move the Previous Question' is equivalent to a proposal 'That the question be not put, ever' and that phrase is sometimes used. Fortunately Chair may refuse to accept it, most people will not have met it previously so Chair would need to explain how drastic it is and even the proposer may have second thoughts and withdraw it as she is always allowed to do. If accepted and seconded it must be put immediately to vote without more ado. The result is likely to be disruptive either way. If defeated, the subject of that Motion must be immediately put to the vote with no further discussion, amendment or adjournment. If carried, the original motion must at the very least be significantly re-worded for it must never again come before that group in that form. It is an extreme measure, almost never encountered and to be avoided at almost all costs.

Checklist of Preparations for an AGM
This is usually the responsibility of the Hon Secretary. Most arrangements will be as for a normal discussion or for a 'speaker' meeting but with several extras, some required by the Rules. Much will actually be done by other people but you should check that everything necessary has, in fact, been done.

Long before the AGM Book the room for the date required by Rules or custom then you can announce at least the date, time and place in the next available circularisation so that the Rules will have been complied with.

Much nearer the time Give a reminder of date and place and request nominations for officers and Committee, stating the vacancies. If it is part of the routine of your group, ask for Motions and Amendments.

After the last date for Nominations Discuss with Chair and Returning Officer where elections should be placed in the Agenda. Remind any officers who will, or might, be leaving office to check over their papers and books against their list (of which you should have a copy). These should be ready for handing over quietly and without ceremony after the meeting has been declared closed.

Soon before the meeting or at it Supply members with Agenda sheets, Statements of Accounts, Reports of Hon Treasurer and Hon Secretary if these are printed. If they are not, arrange to collect each Report after it has been read out, for filing as part of the Minutes. Publish a final list of nominations either on a blackboard at the meeting or printed and possibly accompanied by a CV (curriculum vitae or 'life history') for each nominee. If relevant, offer the final wordings of Motions to be presented for debate.

On the day itself Check that the Minutes of the previous AGM are available and also those of any Special General Meeting held during that year. Also the rough notes taken at each of them and the rough notes and Minutes of the first Committee meeting after each Special General Meeting when the drafts of the Minutes were discussed and the files of AGM Reports which are, in essence, part of the Minutes sequence, with markers in all the relevant pages. Read through the Minutes to be presented. Some matters may have changed and some pronounciations need rehearsal.

On the Chair's desk Have here a copy of the Rules, Standing Orders and any other controlling papers; instructions to Tellers; spares of all papers concerning the AGM which have been sent or given to members with notes of any recent modifications or amendments; a copy of the Treasurer's list of material assets; a conspicuous note of the date, ready to add to the signature accepting the Minutes and, possibly a pen.

Make sure there is a particularly detailed Chair's Agenda (and try to amend it during the meeting if, for example, Tellers have been unexpectedly appointed). If the Secretary's Report does not include a full list of Officers' Aides or people responsible for particular jobs, include these not only so that they get thanked but to be certain that a full and correct list will be available in the Minutes if needed and to make sure that the books or objects attached to jobs do not get 'lost' over the years.

For each Teller Supply the sheet of Chair's instructions, a bowl to collect Voting papers, blank paper of suitable sizes for writing of a few names; spare paper for their own checklists and larger pieces of thick paper for handing results to Chair. If so planned, arrange for a blackboard and rubber. Set aside somewhere for the Tellers where their quiet talk will not disturb the meeeting but where, if they are members, they can watch progress.

Miscellaneous points If any platform people are retiring, try to keep a few front row chairs empty for them.

If there has been a local emergency such as flooding, count the arrivals of voting members to make sure there is a quorum.

Conducting the meeting

All responsibility lies with whoever is chairing the meeting. Some small groups who have a President appointed *ex officio* sometimes state in their Rules that the President's one duty is the chairing of the AGM. The presence of a 'name' may bring kudos, though this is rather wasted when no non-members are likely to be present and is apt to cause general worry, for however experienced she may be as a Chair, without detailed and up-to-the-minute knowledge of the working of that group she is not likely to recognise all possible pitfalls. With luck, she will be tactful enough to recognise this and simply express her appreciation of the welcome you have given her, then ask you, as Committee Chair, to take over the running of the meeting.

Your Committee has been working with you for a year and you will have discussed with them the details of the day's plans so unless there are unexpected fireworks, everything should go smoothly.

The room should have been prepared well in time and you and your Committee should all have arrived early and be moving socially among the people present. This matters. Well organised members who are too busy to attend many meetings try to get at least to the AGM and this may be a rare opportunity for you to welcome some of your more influential members. Keep looking as unhurried and unworried as any good hostess should. When you know you have a quorum the last of your preliminary worries ought to be over and, by the scheduled time, everyone should be settled in her place, members with balance sheets, lists of nominations, Agenda sheets etc, and officers and Committee members with papers checked and ready to start on Item 1 of the Agenda.

1) Welcome by the Chair On the dot if possible, you should rise and welcome everyone. Then leave it at that. You are simply demonstrating that the meeting has started and in an unfamiliar room you may be testing the acoustics.

2) Apologies for absence Such long notice has been given for this highlight of the year's activities that established members are not likely to be absent without good reason so apologies deserve to be read out. They might signal movement or illness.

3) Minutes of the 12th (or whichever) AGM held on . . . A year is a long time and even those who were at the meeting are often surprised by what was apparently done then. Few have the confidence to challenge the record but if they do, you need not worry. The Minutes' accuracy was vouched for at the Committee held when memories were still fresh and the Minutes recording this are available. When you ask that the Minutes should be accepted, anyone may propose or second but as you survey the raised hands, try to catch the eye and call the name of established members of the group who are not Committee members. Then don't forget to ask the meeting to show they agree that the Minutes be accepted. Sign and date them. Do the same with the Minutes of any Special General Meeting there may have been. They are all now part of the history of the group.

4) Matters arising from the Minutes This item is rarely needed for almost everything should have been dealt with during the year and the rest should come into Reports. In fact, 'Business Arising' is often omitted from an AGM Agenda but meetings go better if an item is scheduled but not needed, than they do if there is something which ought to be said but nowhere to say it.

5) Appointment of Tellers If there are no elections you can simply say 'I am sorry that this year there are no elections so there seems to be no need for Tellers' and move to the next item, but beware of implying that the absence of elections is to be welcomed. Maybe it does save immediate bother but if it is seen to be welcomed, nominators may start to get a disgruntled feeling that 'it's all organised and they don't want us butting in'.

The exact placing of the item, though necessarily before the elections, is not important but if the tellers are elected early, they can settle down and consider how best to do their job. Also, a Chair should always have a 'runner' available and Tellers are ideal.

6) 7) and 8) Reports If these are read out, give time for them to be collected for filing. AGM Reports become part of the group's history when accepted by the members so when you have answered any questions about yours, which is a personal review, ask for someone to propose that it has been received and considered (that is, that members know and accept its contents). Proposer and seconder are sure to be forthcoming and their names must be Minuted, for Reports matter. Ask for a show of hands to demonstrate that the meeting as a whole accepts your Report into the records.

Use a slightly different phrase in dealing with the Reports of Treasurer and Secretary for theirs are statistical, not personal. Their accuracy might be in question so Chair needs to ask not only that they be received and considered but that they be adopted. Anyone (except its giver) may propose the acceptance of any report but as the activities are supposed to be carried out on the instructions of the Committee, it is tactful for those who serve on that Committee to leave these various proposings and secondings to others.

9) Appointment of Auditor To make sure there is no hint of collusion between Auditor and Treasurer, this item is basically yours to deal with, not hers, even though you may have never met that Auditor. Don't let this item slip by without proper acknowledgement. One of the most responsible jobs, whether or not it was done without charge, should not be allowed to go almost unremarked simply because, by definition, it is done by an outsider. Take this opportunity to thank her properly and ask the agreement of the meeting that a letter should be sent by you or by the Hon Secretary, quoting the thanks the Hon Treasurer offered in her Report. If you know that the Auditor is willing to act again and is wanted, the thanks can be linked with this invitation. If, for any reason, a change has to be made, the Committee should already have put forward the name of someone of repute and skill but if this could not be done, probably some experienced person will propose, from the floor, that the matter be left in the hands of the Committee. If, however, members suspect that all is not well, they would be quite within their rights to insist that another meeting be called for the specific purpose of considering this matter, or any other aspect of finances. It should be remarked that no financial Resolution should ever be passed which has not appeared in some form on the Agenda.

10) Elections There is always restlessness until these are over, so get on with them as soon as possible. If several stages are needed, carry on with the business between whiles; if only one stage is needed you may, but need not, give your members a break to talk and move about.

11) and onward Business characteristic of the group and special motions As well as their own special business, small groups often consider the possibility of a change in their own Rules or may wish to make suggestions which might have wider outside effects. All such need to be backed by the full authority of at least a Special but preferably an Annual General Meeting. Larger organisations do this regularly, usually at Conferences with a General Meeting later, not to re-hash the debate but to decide whether or not to take official responsibility for the Resolutions and if so to whom they will direct them.

Final item, AOB It is easy for you to feel that, bar fireworks, the busines of the meeting is virtually over but don't relax yet or the thanks which make up most of this item will be less than heartfelt.

Just occasionally, someone puts forward some detailed suggestion for the planning of the next year, forgetting that the old Committee has only a few more minutes of authority and the new Committee doesn't yet know its own mind, not having met. Let her speak and be Minuted. Ask her to write to someone on the new Committee to start further discussions. Suggestions should always be welcomed and when the Minutes are read next year, all will know whether it was a bad idea which ran into the sand or something brilliant has come of the suggestion. Finally, thank all who have helped on the day, including those who have helped all year. Chair's Agenda should have all the names.

All else done, if you are continuing in office, declare the meeting closed. If you are leaving it and the group has a badge of office, prepare to pass it to your successor, welcoming her while doing so and wishing her well in her term of office. Then sweep your papers together and go and sit with the other departing officers among the members and leave the meeting in your successor's hands. Her speech must be short, for until her Committee has met there is little she can say, but she will probably wish to express her appreciation of your work and welcome her new Committee, which she may ask to assemble in a few moments to discuss the meeting dates for the year — and the sooner they meet the better.

If the Agenda has listed the change of Chairmanship as after the AGM, you will already have closed the meeting before your successor speaks, but if it is listed as part of the final item, it is for her to make the closure. She might then give out any non-AGM notices which may have come in at the last moment.

It used to be normal after the end of business for an older member to make an entirely unscheduled speech from the floor praising the skill of whoever Chaired the meeting. This is becoming less usual but if it happens to you, enjoy it. You probably deserve it.

In some groups it is the custom for the incumbent Committee to continue in office until a date stated in the Rules and always the same, year by year. For these, the AGM itself usually ends with no more ceremony than an invitation from the Chairman to the Committee elect to join the incumbent Committee at its final meeting(s). The change-over then happens at a Committee meeting rather than at the AGM and is in some ways much smoother and easier, though duller if the group happens to hanker for ceremony.

In a very few groups the change takes place progressively throughout the AGM, each officer, as her election is announced, taking the place of her predecessor and claiming the books and papers left ready for her. This has the very real disadvantage of causing fuss and movement which might continue throughout the meeting. Also, the meeting itself cannot be planned, for at least in theory and sometimes in practice no-one can tell until the elections have been held who will be running the later items. Also, under this arrangement an officer dealing with an activity she is known to disapprove of may find herself in the awkward position of having to defend it if it comes into a discussion after her election. Fortunately, this routine is rarely advocated.

Even when the new 'reign' has begun a few jobs remain which someone must organise. The results of elections must be sent to any advertising and information points, such as the local library and to the local papers, which, outside big conurbations, are always avid for such information. Branch representatives need also to inform HQ.

CLOSING A GROUP

However regrettable the need for this, *branches of organisations* should not find the routine puzzling, for their HQ should tell them what it wishes them to do. Usually it will expect any money to be returned to the central office, for almost certainly they advanced money to help form the branch, however long ago. Books and papers usually go back to HQ as part of the archives of the organisation, money for postage being taken from the residual funds, the entry being made in the cash book before final totalling and packing. The Minutes of the final AGM or SGM, written up while the meeting was in progress, should be read, accepted and signed before that meeting disperses.

Local groups make their own routine. If any money remains it will probably be devoted to some local good work or memorial or even to a final fling. Records have local historical importance and should be offered to the archives office, museum or library.

When the archievement of its aim (the play was put on, the footpath made safe for posterity) is the cause of the closure of the group, all will rejoice in the success but those who have succeeded in one task are better equipped than most to succeed at another. Members of a group who have fulfilled an aim will most likely wish to start on a new crusade and decide to turn over the page of the record books with full ceremony, write fresh headings, officially make over all money and material assets from one set of accounts to another, re-examine the title of the proposed successor group and start compiling a fresh set of Rules ready to achieve new goals.

INDEX